T0158885

hype

an Ayahuasca Journey

Carla Mora

BALBOA.
PRESS

A DIVISION OF HAY HOUSE

Balboa Press books may be ordered through booksellers or by contacting:

Balboa Press
A Division of Hay House
1663 Liberty Drive
Bloomington, IN 47403
www.balboapress.com
1 (877) 407-4847

Because of the dynamic nature of the Internet, any web addresses or links contained in this book may have changed since publication and may no longer be valid. The views expressed in this work are solely those of the author and do not necessarily reflect the views of the publisher, and the publisher hereby disclaims any responsibility for them.

The author of this book does not dispense medical advice or prescribe the use of any technique as a form of treatment for physical, emotional, or medical problems without the advice of a physician, either directly or indirectly. The intent of the author is only to offer information of a general nature to help you in your quest for emotional and spiritual well-being. In the event you use any of the information in this book for yourself, which is your constitutional right, the author and the publisher assume no responsibility for your actions.

Any people depicted in stock imagery provided by Thinkstock are models, and such images are being used for illustrative purposes only.
Certain stock imagery © Thinkstock.

Print information available on the last page.

ISBN: 978-1-5043-7572-6 (sc)
ISBN: 978-1-5043-7573-3 (e)

Library of Congress Control Number: 2017903228

Balboa Press rev. date: 03/25/2017

For Pa

"No human words can prepare one for reality."

Carla's subconscious?
Mother Ayahuasca?
Carla's "higher self"?
Your guess is as good as mine ...

Introduction

Dear reader, fellow human, brother, sister,

I love you.

I am sharing this journal, a record of part of my journey, which helped me with my beloved's journey. My boyfriend Shem ("Pa") transitioned in June 2016. He had cancer. I went on a twelve-day shamanic cleanse retreat, returning in September 2, 2015. Around then he started exhibiting symptoms of the disease. It was not until December 24, 2015 that he was diagnosed with stage IV colon cancer, at the age of thirty-three.

The next seven months were grueling, as we scrambled to find a way to heal my beloved. He was in excruciating pain and suffered from sleep deprivation and fatigue, while having to make difficult decisions. Initially, he chose chemotherapy at one of the top-rated facilities in the United States. We were told his cancer was incurable and he would need chemo for the rest of his life, however long that might be. It was nearly impossible to keep up with chemotherapy, drugs, many side effects, homeopathic treatments, mental care and support, and chasing the latest cancer-fighting treatment. After seven debilitating chemo treatments, we travelled to Mexico, for treatment at a clinic offering alternative treatments not available in the States. We were devastated to hear that the Mexican clinic suggested he get chemo, in addition to their treatments. Cannabis oil was the next course of treatment we would try when we returned to America, in addition to the Mexican treatments. We were having success with dosing cannabis oil, until a blood clot was found, in addition to battling lymphedema, which forced him into two different hospital stays.

It's hard to tell for certain, but it is my belief that chemotherapy advanced his cancer and caused more damage than good.

It was excruciating and heart wrenching to watch his health decline. Unfortunately, many of you know from experience, and for that I am sorry. No one should have to go through any of it: patient, caregiver, or family. I am grateful beyond words that I experienced the healing and teaching of this powerful medicine plant, Ayahuasca. I am grateful for the facilitators, shaman, helpers, and fellow journeymen.

I am grateful because the medicine, whose teaching and healing is powerful and effective, helped me navigate the worst of experiences; somehow, it made some parts tolerable and others even beautiful. The medicine seems to guide the way, but the individual must do work. This book is shared in hopes that if you are curious and seek healing, perhaps you will gain knowledge enough to experience it yourself. I do believe in the concept that if you heal yourself, you heal the world.

A portion of the proceeds of the purchase from this book will be donated to people who want to experience this journey and can't afford it. Thank you for helping with that.

Before I left for Peru, I let Pa know that I would only communicate with him through writing in this journal. I said that I would not email, text, or call for the fourteen days I was away. If I had anything to say to him, I would write it in the journal. The journal is not edited and contains a ton of errors and so, to those who cringe at seeing grammatical errors, I apologize. I am very thankful Pa asked me to read the journal to him because he is one of those people.

I named the book *hype* because there is a lot of hype about Mama Ayahuasca. Some hype is positive and some hype is negative, and some is simply untrue. I published this book to hype my experience and encourage people not to believe any of the hype but to become curious enough to find out for themselves.

Some know of Mama Ayahuasca through Joe Rogan or Robin Quivers of *The Howard Stern Show*. It has been talked about on television shows and in movies. After my experience, I saw it portrayed terribly in a movie on my flight home from Peru. There may very well be experiences that look just like that, but there are others which are beautiful and life changing, when guidance and information is given along with the medicine. People experience the medicine differently.

Peru was calling me. I had a strong pull toward this experience. Prior to the trip, on the weekend of July 4, I had an emergency appendectomy. Because of that, I found the courage to ask for the time off work and take a chance on doing something out of the ordinary because surgery was pretty scary, but successful. I wanted to live in a more meaningful way, and this shamanic cleanse seemed like a great catalyst, a new beginning.

I would like to thank Jon Allen for his contributions to this project. He did an outstanding job photographing the images and drawing the artwork border for the images.

Thank you to those who supported Pa and me through all of this. I am extremely blessed and grateful.

Thank you for those who nudged me to do this.

I have written that something "is" for Pa, rather than "was," in many places. I still feel him with me, so I can't help but write it that way. Also, I wrote some notes, which you will find in the back of the book, to help explain inside jokes, some of my views that have changed since the trip, apologies, and more.

I love you.

Ma

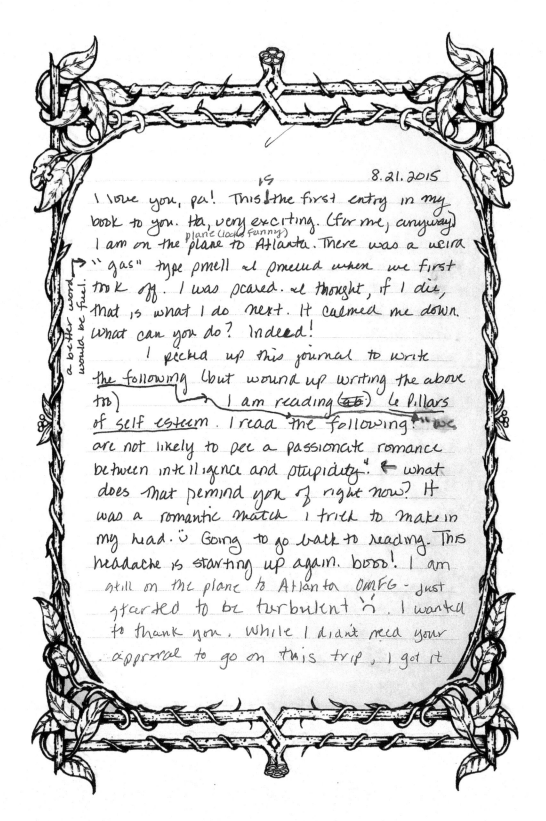

8.21.2015

I love you, pa! This the first entry in my book to you. Ha, very exciting. (for me, anyway)
I am on the plane (looks funny) to Atlanta. There was a weird "gas" type smell I smelled when we first took off. I was scared. I thought, if I die, that is what I do next. It calmed me down. What can you do? Indeed!

I picked up this journal to write the following (but wound up writing the above too) → I am reading ~~the~~ le Pillars of self esteem. I read the following: "we are not likely to see a passionate romance between intelligence and stupidity." ← what does that remind you of right now? It was a romantic match I tried to make in my head. ☺ Going to go back to reading. This headache is starting up again. booo! I am still on the plane to Atlanta OMFG - just started to be turbulent ☹. I wanted to thank you. While I didn't need your approval to go on this trip, I got it

a better word would be fuel.

1

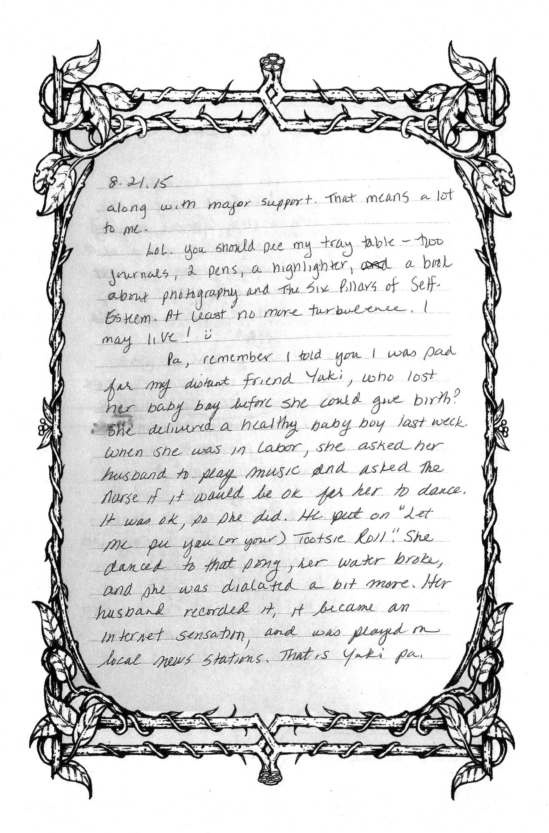

8.21.15

along with major support. That means a lot
to me.

LoL. you should see my tray table — two
journals, 2 pens, a highlighter, and a book
about photography and The six Pillars of Self-
Esteem. At least no more turbulence. I
may live! ü

Pa, remember I told you I was sad
for my distant friend Yuki, who lost
her baby boy before she could give birth?
She delivered a healthy baby boy last week.
when she was in labor, she asked her
husband to play music and asked the
Nurse if it would be ok for her to dance.
It was ok, so she did. He put on "Let
me see you (or your) Tootsie Roll." She
danced to that song, her water broke,
and she was dialated a bit more. Her
husband recorded it, it became an
internet sensation, and was played on
local news stations. That is Yuki pa.

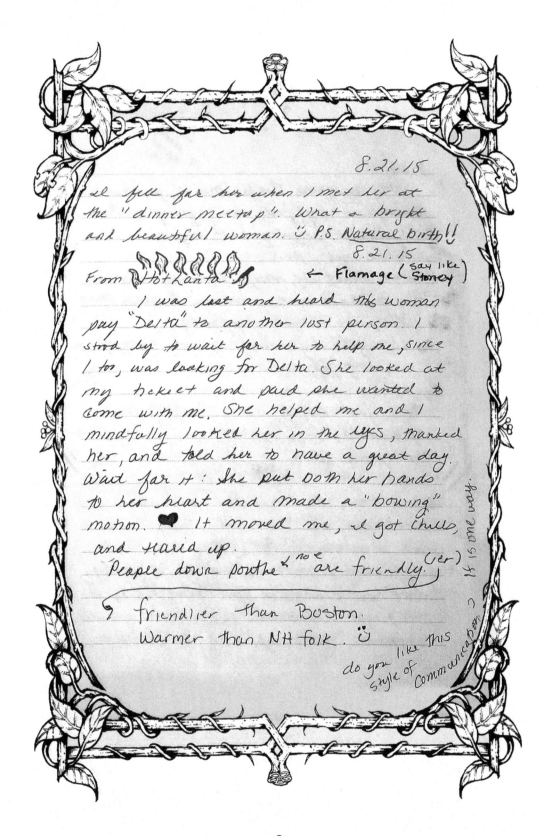

8.21.15

I fell for her when I met her at the "dinner meetup". What a bright and beautiful woman. ☺ P.S. Natural birth!!

8.21.15

From ⟪HotLanta⟫ ← Flamage (say like Stoney)

I was lost and heard this woman say "Delta" to another lost person. I stood by to wait for her to help me, since I too, was looking for Delta. She looked at my ticket and said she wanted to come with me. She helped me and I mindfully looked her in the eyes, thanked her, and told her to have a great day. Wait for it: She put both her hands to her heart and made a "bowing" motion. ❤ It moved me, I got chills, and teared up.

"People down southe^(no c) are friendly. (ier)

Friendlier than Boston. Warmer than NH folk. ☺

do you like this style of communication?

It is one way.

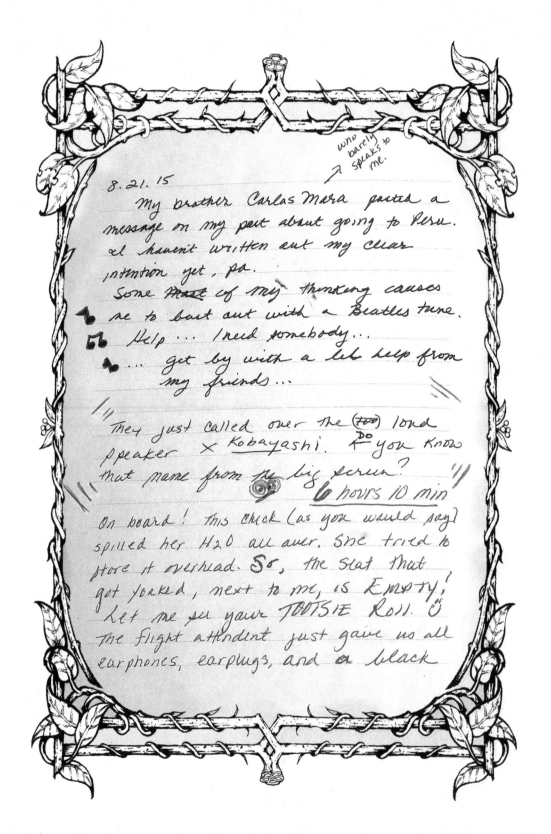

8.21.15

My brother Carlos Mara posted a
message on my post about going to Peru.
I haven't written out my clear
intention yet, pa.

Some ~~most~~ of my thinking causes
me to bust out with a Beatles tune.

♪ Help ... I need somebody...

♪ ... get by with a lil help from
my friends ...

They just called over the (~~too~~) loud
speaker ✗ <u>Kobayashi</u>. ^{Do} you know
that name from ~~the~~ big screen?

6 hours 10 min

On board! This chick (as you would say)
spilled her H₂0 all over. She tried to
store it overhead. So, the seat that
got yonked, next to me, is EMPTY!
Let me see your TOOTSIE Roll. ☺
The flight attendent just gave us all
earphones, earplugs, and ~~a~~ black

who barely speaks to me.

4

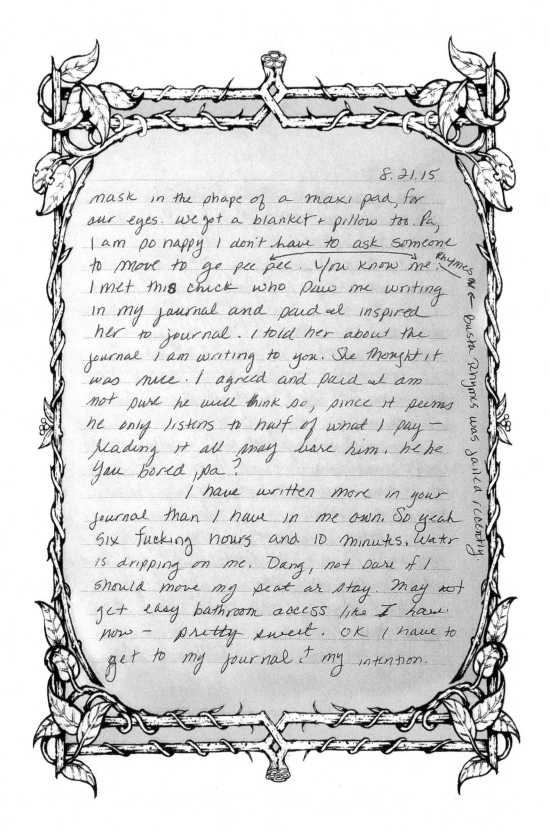

8.21.15

mask in the shape of a maxi pad, for
our eyes. We get a blanket + pillow too. Pa,
I am so happy I don't have to ask someone
to move to go pee pee. You know me. Rhymes M←
I met this chick who saw me writing
in my journal and said it inspired
her to journal. I told her about the
journal I am writing to you. She thought it
was nice. I agreed and said I am
not sure he will think so, since it seems
he only listens to half of what I say —
reading it all may bore him. He he
You bored, pa?
          I have written more in your
journal than I have in me own. So yeah
Six fucking hours and 10 minutes. Water
is dripping on me. Dang, not sure if I
should move my seat or stay. May not
get easy bathroom access like I have
now — pretty sweet. OK I have to
get to my journal + my intention.

← Busta Rhymes was said relating.

5

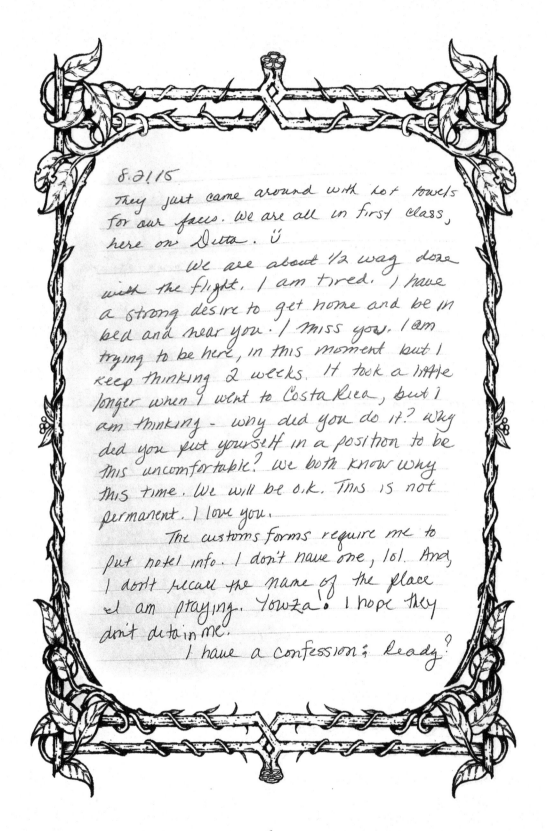

8.2.15

They just came around with hot towels for our faces. We are all in first class, here on Delta. ☺

We are about ½ way done with the flight. I am tired. I have a strong desire to get home and be in bed and near you. I miss you. I am trying to be here, in this moment but I keep thinking 2 weeks. It took a little longer when I went to Costa Rica, but I am thinking - why did you do it? why did you put yourself in a position to be this uncomfortable? We both know why this time. We will be o.k. This is not permanent. I love you.

The customs forms require me to put hotel info. I don't have one, lol. And, I don't recall the name of the place I am staying. Yowza! I hope they don't detain me.

I have a confession: Ready?

8.21.15

I was on the verge of asking you if we
could get a dog. It would have to be a
little dog - that is the kicker and why
I never asked. We can't have a dog -
Yet.

8.22.15

Papa, I am in Lima, Peru. It's just after
1°°am and I am chilling (literally, cause these
tiles are cold) on the floor at the airport. I am
reading the complicated book on photography.
I must be patient because there is much
to learn. It can be overwhelming, esp.
with all of these new (to me) terms. I am
a little lonely. Some people who are on the
floor are cuddled up with one another. I
told you, you are like home, so I would
feel so much better @ home. ↙ if you were
here - in case you didn't get that. There
are many other lone travellers, like
me. Some of these people look like
they are pure indigenous Andean

I mean the   ↖ I may h
wording. ↙ here   made
                     up.

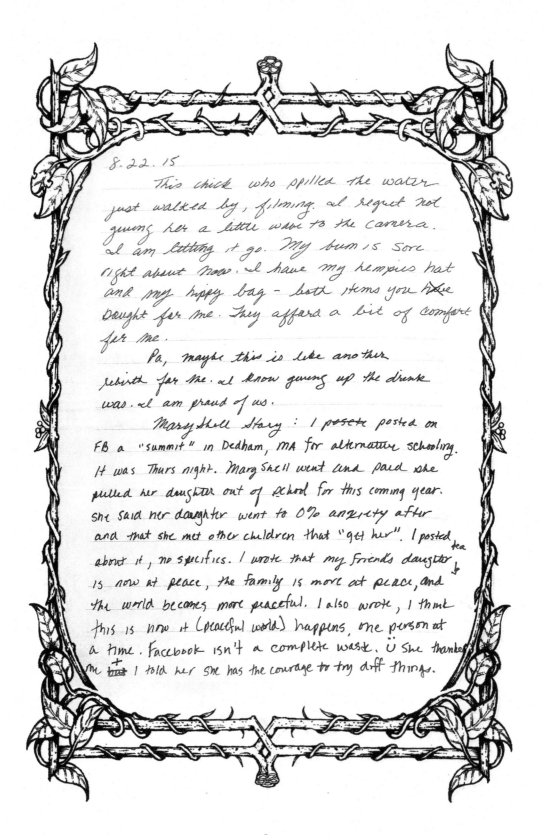

8.22.15

This chick who spilled the water just walked by, filming. I regret not giving her a little wave to the camera. I am letting it go. My bum is sore right about now. I have my hempies hat and my hippy bag — both items you bought for me. They afford a bit of comfort for me.

Pa, maybe this is like another rebirth for me. I know giving up the drink was. I am proud of us.

Mary Shell Story : I posted on FB a "summit" in Dedham, MA for alternative schooling. It was Thurs night. Mary Shell went and paid she pulled her daughter out of school for this coming year. She said her daughter went to 0% anxiety after and that she met other children that "get her". I posted about it, no specifics. I wrote that my friend's daughter is now at peace, the family is more at peace, and the world becomes more peaceful. I also wrote, I think this is how it (peaceful world) happens, one person at a time. Facebook isn't a complete waste. ü She thanked me and I told her she has the courage to try diff things.

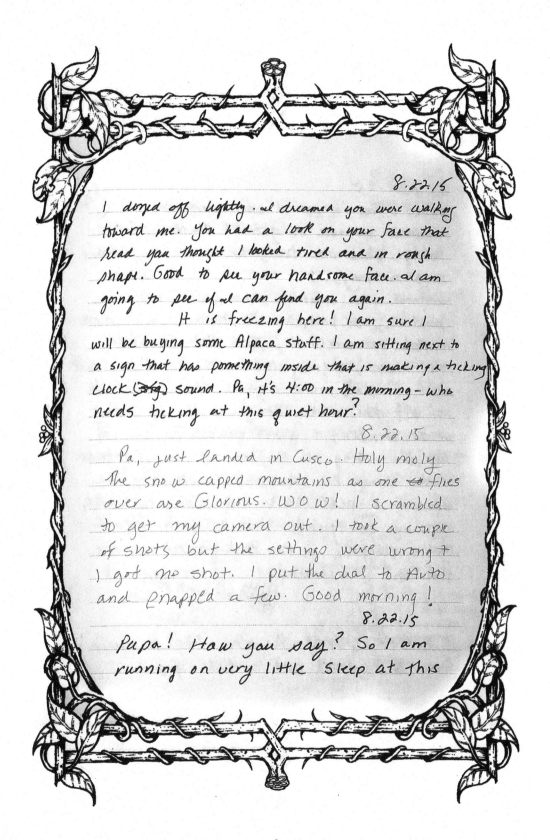

8.22.15

I dozed off lightly. I dreamed you were walking toward me. You had a look on your face that read you thought I looked tired and in rough shape. Good to see your handsome face. I am going to see if I can find you again.

It is freezing here! I am sure I will be buying some Alpaca stuff. I am sitting next to a sign that has something inside that is making a ticking clock (~~stq~~) sound. Pa, it's 4:00 in the morning - who needs ticking at this quiet hour?

8.22.15

Pa, just landed in Cusco. Holy moly the snow capped mountains as one ~~to~~ flies over are Glorious. WOW! I scrambled to get my camera out. I took a couple of shots but the settings were wrong + I got no shot. I put the dial to Auto and snapped a few. Good morning!

8.22.15

Pupa! How you say? So I am running on very little sleep at this

9

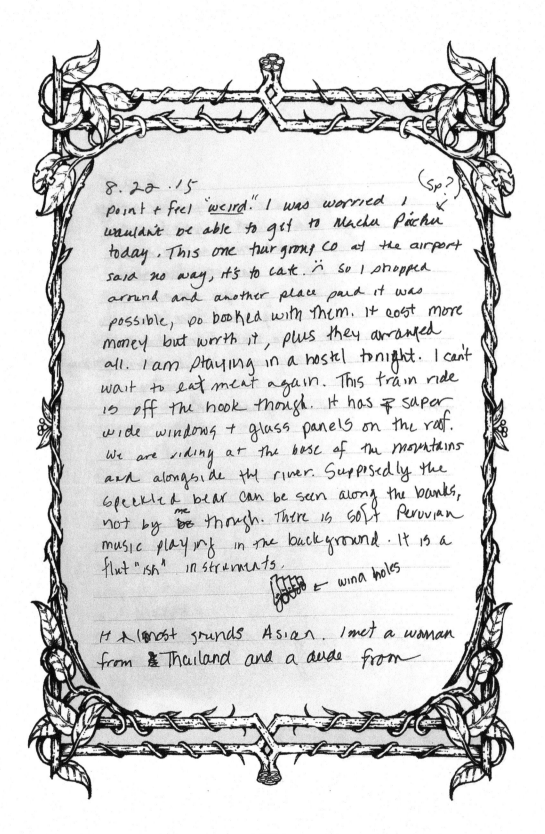

8.22.15   (sp?)

point + feel "weird." I was worried I   &
wouldn't be able to get to Machu Picchu
today. This one tour group Co at the airport
said no way, it's to late." So I shopped
around and another place said it was
possible, so booked with them. It cost more
money but worth it, plus they arranged
all. I am staying in a hostel tonight. I can't
wait to eat meat again. This train ride
is off the hook though. It has a super
wide windows + glass panels on the roof.
We are riding at the base of the mountains
and alongside the river. Supposedly the
speckled bear can be seen along the banks,
not by me though. There is soft Peruvian
music playing in the background. It is a
flut "ish" instruments.
                              ← wind holes

It almost sounds Asian. I met a woman
from Thailand and a dude from

10

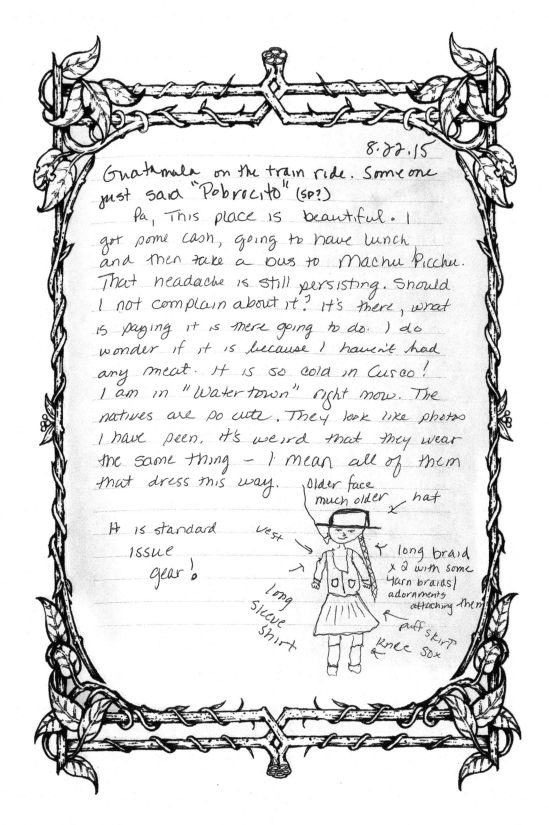

8.27.15

Guatemala on the train ride. Someone just said "Pobrecito" (sp?)

Pa, This place is beautiful. I got some cash, going to have lunch and then take a bus to Machu Picchu. That headache is still persisting. Should I not complain about it? It's there, what is saying it is there going to do. I do wonder if it is because I haven't had any meat. It is so cold in Cusco! I am in "Water town" right now. The natives are so cute. They look like photos I have seen. It's weird that they wear the same thing — I mean all of them that dress this way.

It is standard issue gear!

Older face much older — hat

vest →

long braid x 2 with some yarn braids/ adornments attaching them

long sleeve shirt

puff skirt?

knee sox

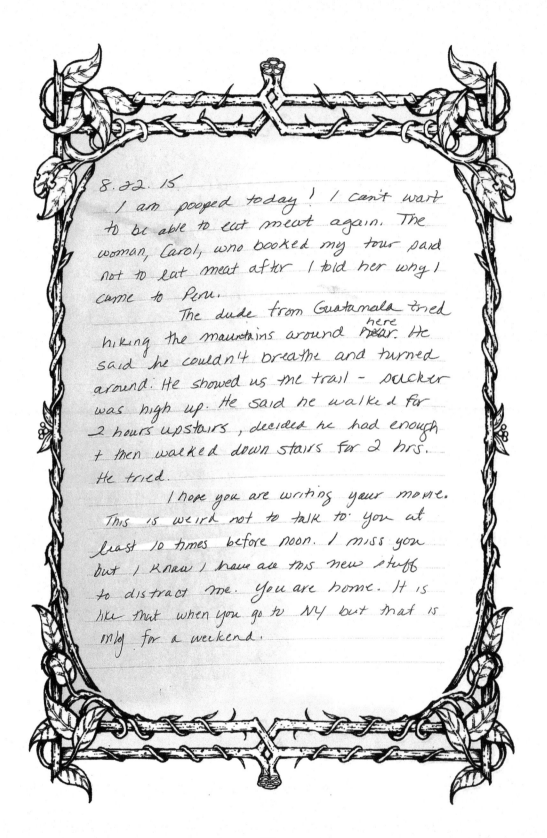

8.22.15.

I am pooped today! I can't wait to be able to eat meat again. The woman, Carol, who booked my tour said not to eat meat after I told her why I came to Peru.

The dude from Guatamala tried hiking the mountains around ~~near~~ here. He said he couldn't breathe and turned around. He showed us the trail — sucker was high up. He said he walked for 2 hours upstairs, decided he had enough + then walked down stairs for 2 hrs. He tried.

I hope you are writing your movie. This is weird not to talk to you at least 10 times before noon. I miss you but I know I have all this new stuff to distract me. You are home. It is like that when you go to NY but that is only for a weekend.

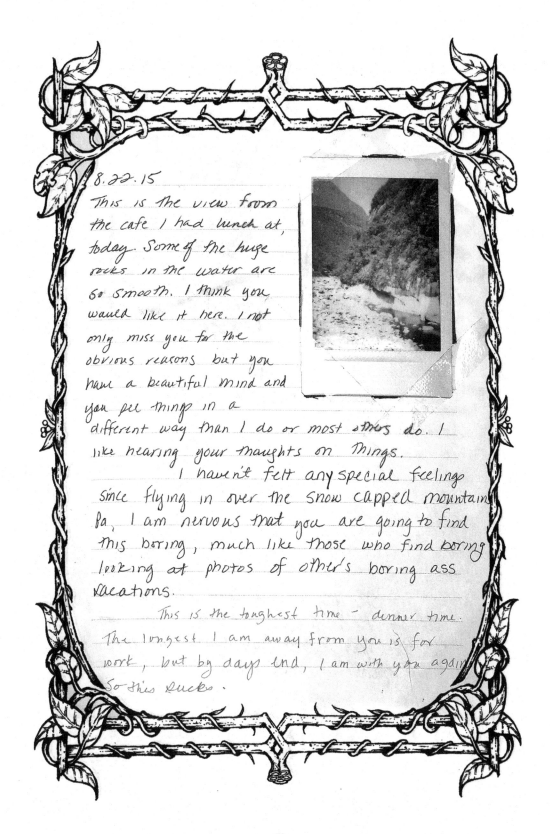

8.22.15

This is the view from the cafe I had lunch at, today. Some of the huge rocks in the water are so smooth. I think you would like it here. I not only miss you for the obvious reasons but you have a beautiful mind and you see things in a different way than I do or most others do. I like hearing your thoughts on things.

I haven't felt any special feelings since flying in over the snow capped mountains Ba, I am nervous that you are going to find this boring, much like those who find boring looking at photos of other's boring ass vacations.

This is the toughest time - dinner time. The longest I am away from you is for work, but by days end, I am with you again. So this sucks.

13

8.22.15

So I just came down from Machu Picchu (correct sp!) It was a sight to behold pa! The shots I took for you didn't come out very well. The animals did. Pa, the selfie sticks were plentiful today. The place is way up. We kept climbing and climbing. I was dishevelled. Some guides are available which I think would make it more interesting. I didn't get a guide. I had a really tough time with the heights. I almost left! Talk about wanting you with me. There are dogs everywhere! Perros. I am eating SOPA... mushroom sopa.

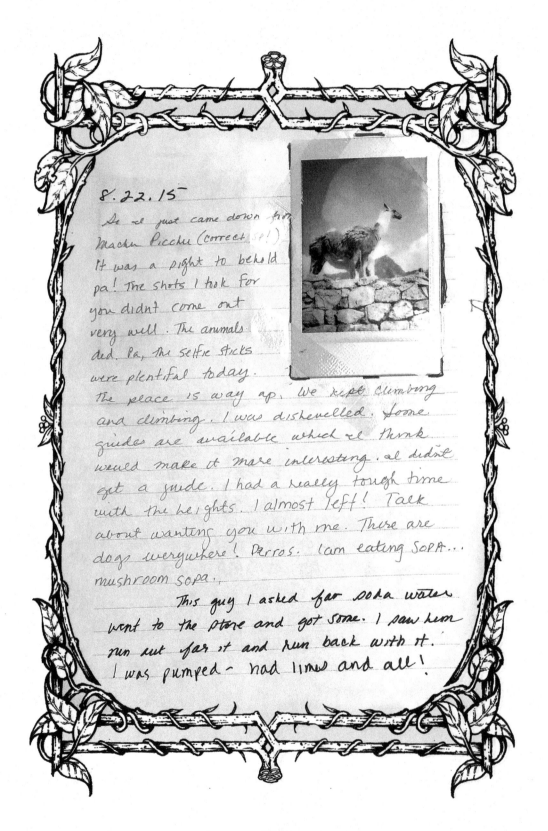

This guy I asked for soda water went to the store and got some. I saw him run out for it and run back with it. I was pumped — had limes and all!

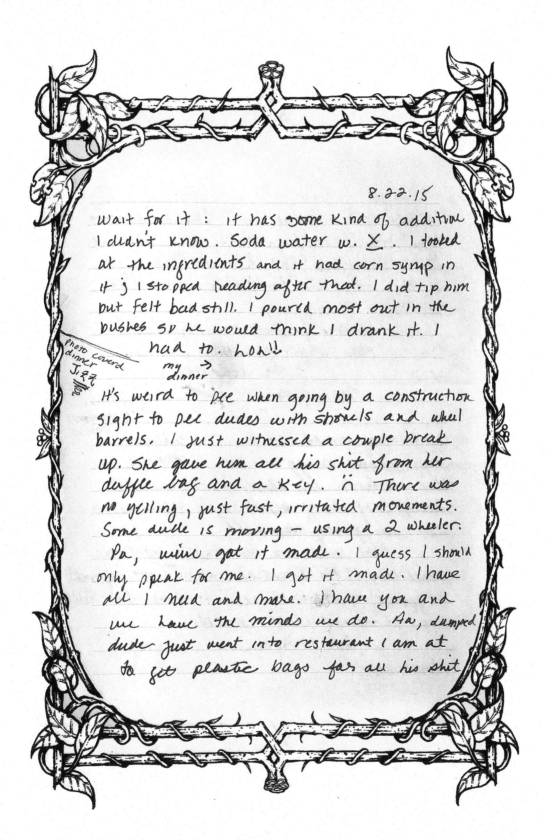

8.22.15

Wait for it : it has some kind of additive
I didn't know. Soda water w. X . I looked
at the ingredients and it had corn syrup in
it ; I stopped reading after that. I did tip him
but felt bad still. I poured most out in the
bushes so he would think I drank it. I
had to. LOL!!

photo covered
dinner
Jizz

my →
dinner

It's weird to pee when going by a construction
sight to pee dudes with shovels and wheel
barrels. I just witnessed a couple break
up. She gave him all his shit from her
duffle bag and a key. ¨ There was
no yelling, just fast, irritated movements.
Some dude is moving — using a 2 wheeler.
Pa, mine got it made. I guess I should
only speak for me. I got it made. I have
all I need and more. I have you and
we have the minds we do. Aw, dumped
dude just went into restaurant I am at
to get plastic bags for all his shit

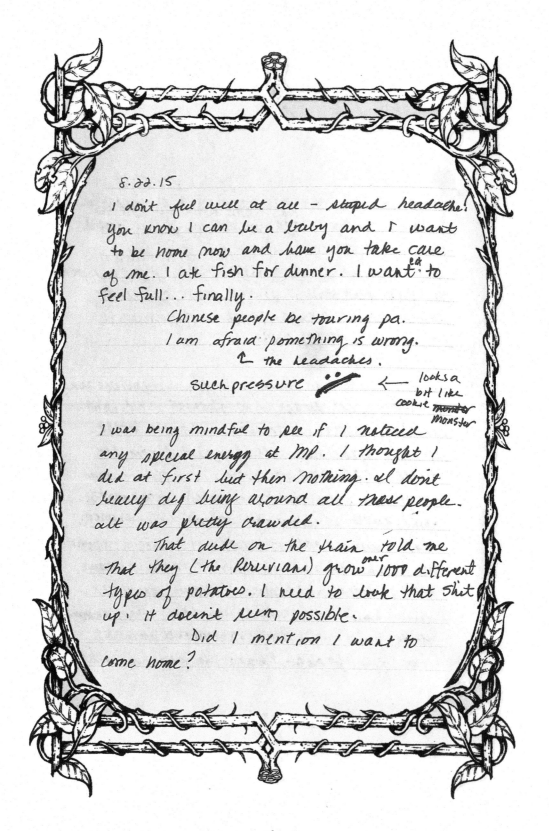

8.22.15

I don't feel well at all – stupid headache!
You know I can be a baby and I want
to be home now and have you take care
of me. I ate fish for dinner. I wanted to
feel full... finally.

Chinese people be touring pa.
I am afraid something is wrong.
↳ the headaches.

such pressure 😶 ← looks a
bit like
cookie ~~monster~~ Monster

I was being mindful to see if I noticed
any special energy at MP. I thought I
did at first but then nothing. I don't
really dig being around all these people.
It was pretty crowded.

That dude on the train told me
that they (the Peruvians) grow over 1000 different
types of potatoes. I need to look that shit
up. It doesn't seem possible.

Did I mention I want to
come home?

16

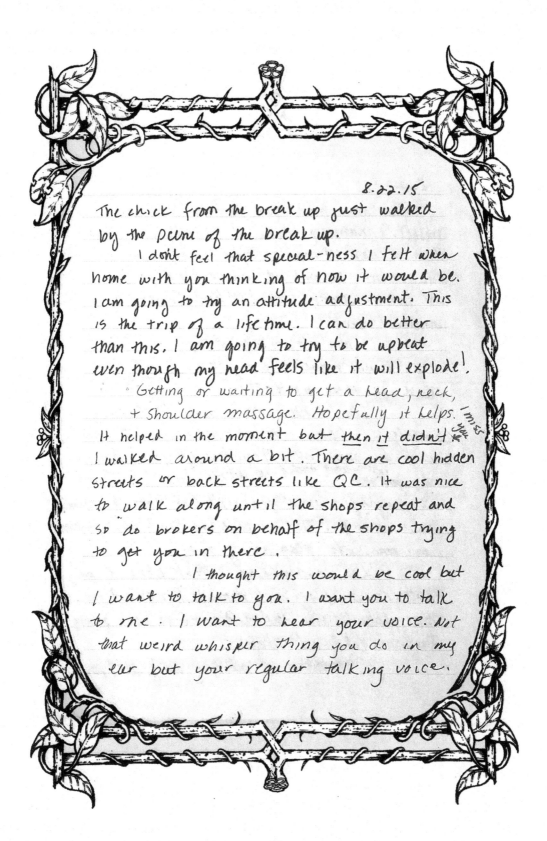

8.22.15

The chick from the break up just walked
by the scene of the break up.

I don't feel that special-ness I felt when
home with you thinking of how it would be.
I am going to try an attitude adjustment. This
is the trip of a life time. I can do better
than this. I am going to try to be upbeat
even though my head feels like it will explode!

Getting or waiting to get a head, neck,
+ shoulder massage. Hopefully it helps. I miss you
It helped in the moment but then it didn't
I walked around a bit. There are cool hidden
streets or back streets like QC. It was nice
to walk along until the shops repeat and
so do brokers on behalf of the shops trying
to get you in there.

I thought this would be cool but
I want to talk to you. I want you to talk
to me. I want to hear your voice. Not
that weird whisper thing you do in my
ear but your regular talking voice.

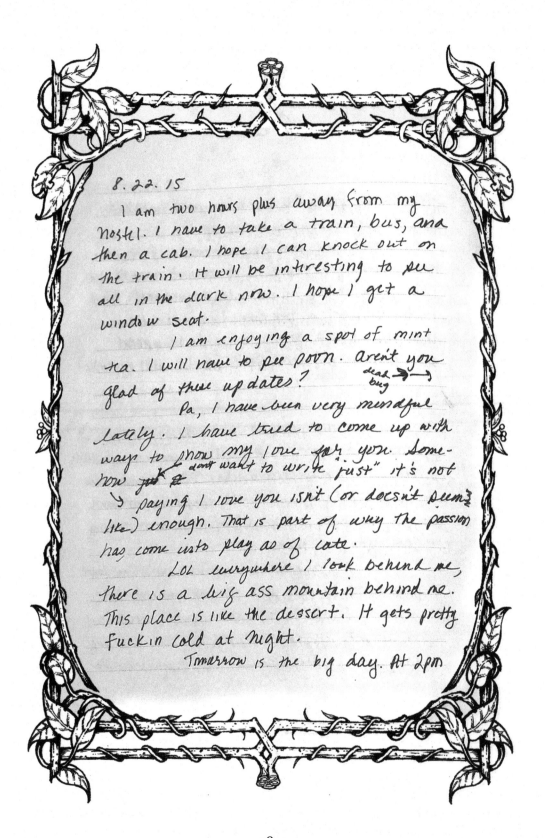

8.22.15

I am two hours plus away from my hostel. I have to take a train, bus, and then a cab. I hope I can knock out on the train. It will be interesting to see all in the dark now. I hope I get a window seat.

    I am enjoying a spot of mint tea. I will have to pee soon. Aren't you glad of these updates? dead bug →

    Pa, I have been very mindful lately. I have tried to come up with ways to show my love for you. Somehow I don't want to write "just" it's not → saying I love you isn't (or doesn't seem like) enough. That is part of why the passion has come into play as of late.

    LOL everywhere I look behind me, there is a big ass mountain behind me. This place is like the dessert. It gets pretty fuckin cold at night.

    Tomorrow is the big day. At 2pm

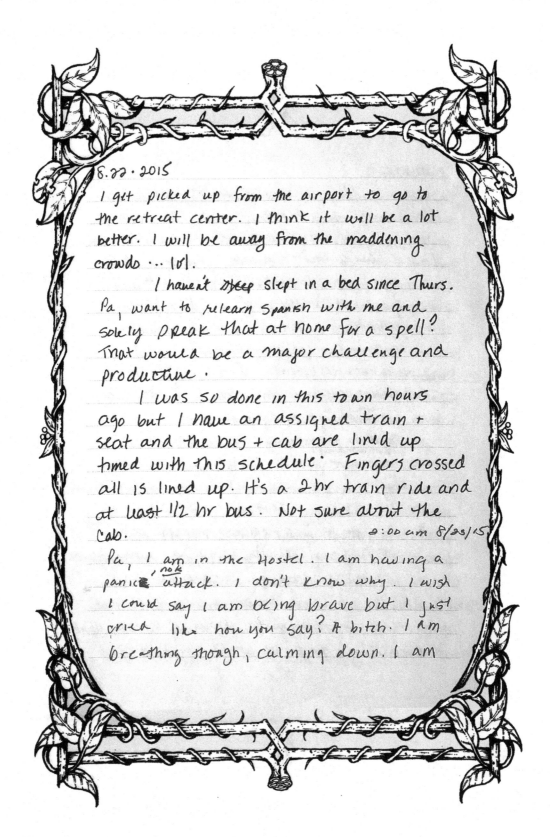

8.22.2015

I get picked up from the airport to go to the retreat center. I think it will be a lot better. I will be away from the maddening crowds ... lol.

I haven't ~~sleep~~ slept in a bed since Thurs. Pa, want to relearn Spanish with me and solely speak that at home for a spell? That would be a major challenge and productive.

I was so done in this town hours ago but I have an assigned train + seat and the bus + cab are lined up timed with this schedule. Fingers crossed all is lined up. It's a 2 hr train ride and at least 1/2 hr bus. Not sure about the cab.

                                     0:00 am 8/23/15

Pa, I am in the Hostel. I am having a panic not attack. I don't know why. I wish I could say I am being brave but I just cried like how you say? A bitch. I am breathing though, calming down. I am

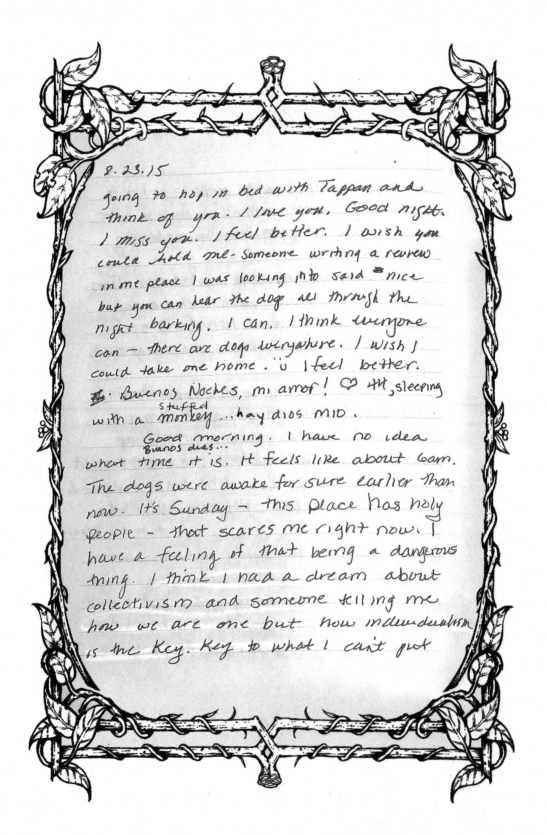

8.23.15

going to hop in bed with Tappan and
think of you. I love you. Good night.
I miss you. I feel better. I wish you
could hold me. Someone writing a review
in one place I was looking into said = nice
but you can hear the dog all through the
night barking. I can. I think everyone
can — there are dogs everywhere. I wish I
could take one home. ☺ I feel better.
🐷 Buenos Noches, mi amor! ♡ 4th, sleeping
with a monkey...hay dios MIO.
          stuffed

        Good morning. I have no idea
        Buenos dias...
what time it is. It feels like about 6am.
The dogs were awake for sure earlier than
now. It's Sunday — this place has holy
people — that scares me right now. I
have a feeling of that being a dangerous
thing. I think I had a dream about
collectivism and someone telling me
how we are one but how individualism
is the key. Key to what I can't put

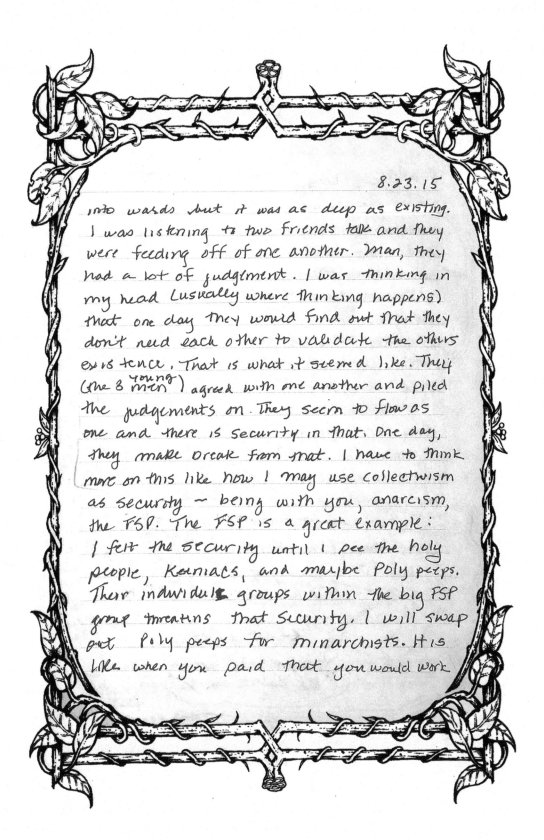

into wards but it was as deep as existing.
I was listening to two friends talk and they
were feeding off of one another. Man, they
had a lot of judgement. I was thinking in
my head (usually where thinking happens)
that one day they would find out that they
don't need each other to validate the others
existence. That is what it seemed like. They
(the 8 young men) agreed with one another and piled
the judgements on. They seem to flow as
one and there is security in that. One day,
they make break from that. I have to think
more on this like how I may use collectivism
as security ~ being with you, anarcism,
the FSP. The FSP is a great example:
I felt the security until I see the holy
people, Keiniacs, and maybe Poly peeps.
Their individual groups within the big FSP
group threatins that security. I will swap
out Poly peeps for minarchists. It is
like when you paid that you would work

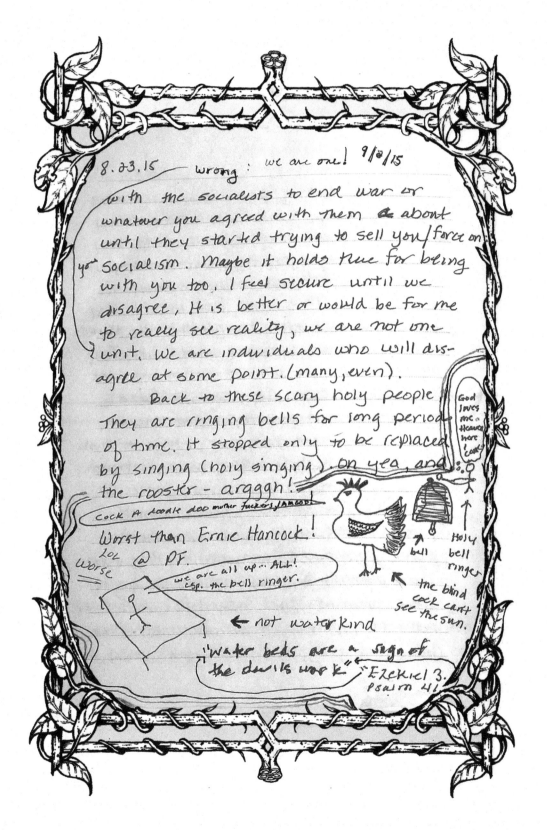

8.23.15   wrong: we are one! 9/2/15

with the socialists to end war or
whatever you agreed with them about
until they started trying to sell you/force on
you socialism. Maybe it holds true for being
with you too. I feel secure until we
disagree. It is better or would be for me
to really see reality, we are not one
unit. We are individuals who will disagree at some point. (many, even).

Back to these scary holy people.
They are ringing bells for long periods
of time. It stopped only to be replaced
by singing (holy singing). Oh yea, and
the rooster - argggh!

COCK A doodle doo mother fuckers, I AM GOD!

Worst than Ernie Hancock!
LOL @ PF.
worse

we are all up.. ALL!
esp. the bell ringer.

← not water kind

"water beds are a sign of
the devils work" Ezekiel 3.
Psalm 41

God
loves
me
Heaven
here
I come

bell

Holy
bell
ringer

the blind
cock cant
see the sun.

22

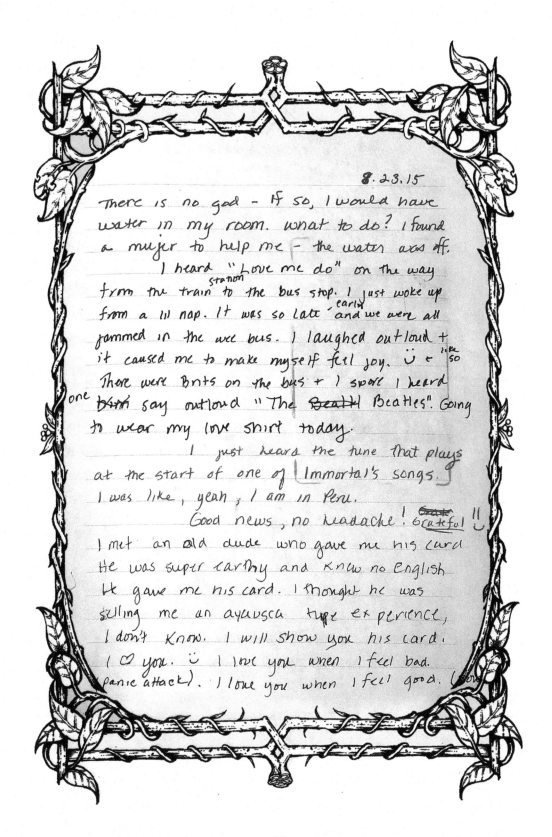

8.23.15

There is no god — If so, I would have
water in my room. What to do? I found
a mujer to help me — the water was off.

I heard "Love me do" on the way
from the train station to the bus stop. I just woke up
from a lil nap. It was so late early and we were all
jammed in the wee bus. I laughed out loud +
it caused me to make myself feel joy. ☺ + like so

There were Brits on the bus + I swore I heard
one say out loud "The Beatl Beatles". Going
to wear my love shirt today.

I just heard the tune that plays
at the start of one of Immortal's songs.
I was like, yeah, I am in Peru.

Good news, no headache! Grateful!! ☺
I met an old dude who gave me his card
He was super earthy and knew no English.
He gave me his card. I thought he was
selling me an ayuasca type experience,
I don't know. I will show you his card.
(♡ you. ☺ I love you when I feel bad.
panic attack). I love you when I feel good. (love

23

This is how is like I say a sentence that sounds like one word.

8.23.15 ↓

I went to went to a farmer's market. It is like that big ass one in Phillie. There are vendors inside and all around on the streets. This one was selling fresh cut pineapple. You know I bought some. Yum. Some dude and I laughed at me because I almost dropped a big piece at one point. I caught it and laughed. The lady next to this lady said 5 Soles for the photo. I gave her $1 and they laughed. Good story for them, maybe? I snapped a photo of her and gave it to her. It is interesting that in a place that is supposed to be a 3rd WC or whatever (U.S. is more developed) they have all this fresh produce + meat so readily available.

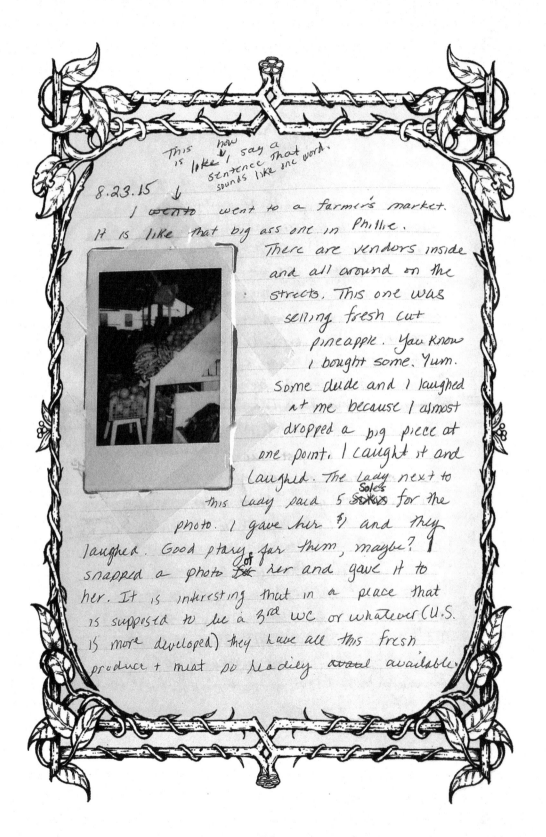

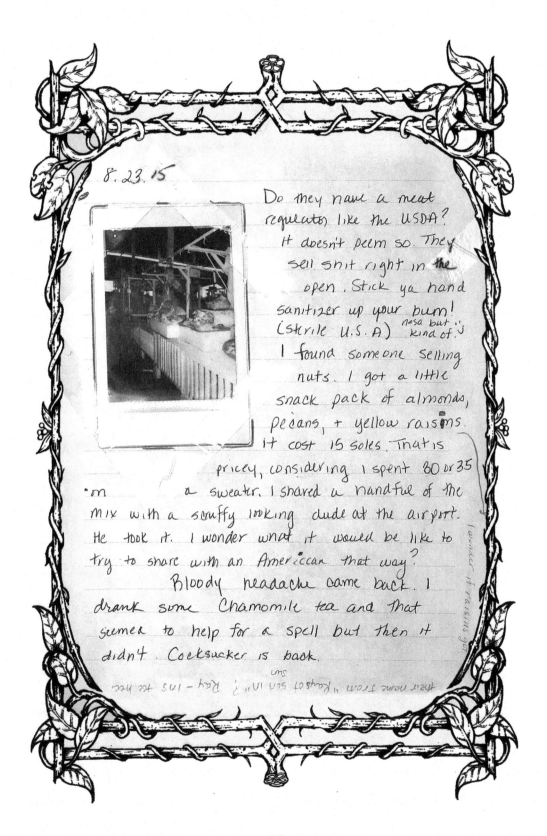

8.23.15

Do they have a meat
regulator like the USDA?
It doesn't seem so. They
sell shit right in the
open. Stick ya hand
sanitizer up your bum!
(sterile U.S.A) ^nasa but kind of.
I found someone selling
nuts. I got a little
snack pack of almonds,
pecans, + yellow raisins.
It cost 15 soles. That is
pricey, considering I spent 30 or 35
on   a sweater. I shared a handful of the
mix with a scruffy looking dude at the airport.
He took it. I wonder what it would be like to
try to share with an American that way?
     Bloody headache came back. I
drank some Chamomile tea and that
seemed to help for a spell but then it
didn't. Cocksucker is back.

their name from "keeps ot sea in", Ray-ins the sea

25

me @ MP

↙ mp

Some other photos
I took @ the
CCHU
They didn't
come out that
good.

8.23.15

Pa, good news, I am going to live! I have altitude sickness. Maybe the headache at home was a premonition. Siracha LoL that isn't the name but it is something close to it is the name in Spanish for it actually. I am ~~Happy~~ relieved that I know what is going on.

Good night, pa! I love you.

Good morning, pa. I went to bed at 8:00pm, so up at the crack ass. The stars were shining bright and now they are not in sight. ~~there are~~ The sky is different hues of blue with a bit of white

The sky is 3x's this but I didn't account for it.

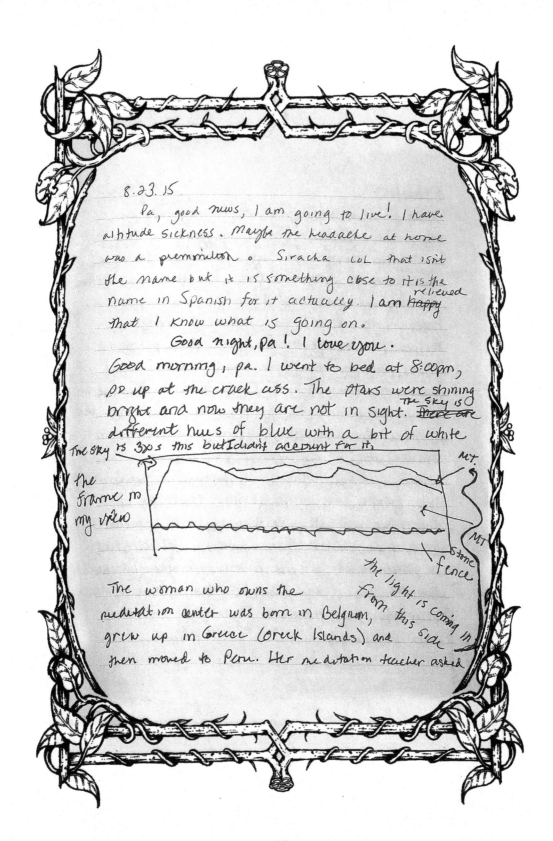

the frame in my view

MT.

MT.

stone fence

The light is coming in from this side

The woman who owns the meditation center was born in Belgium, grew up in Greece (Greek Islands) and then moved to Peru. Her meditation teacher asked

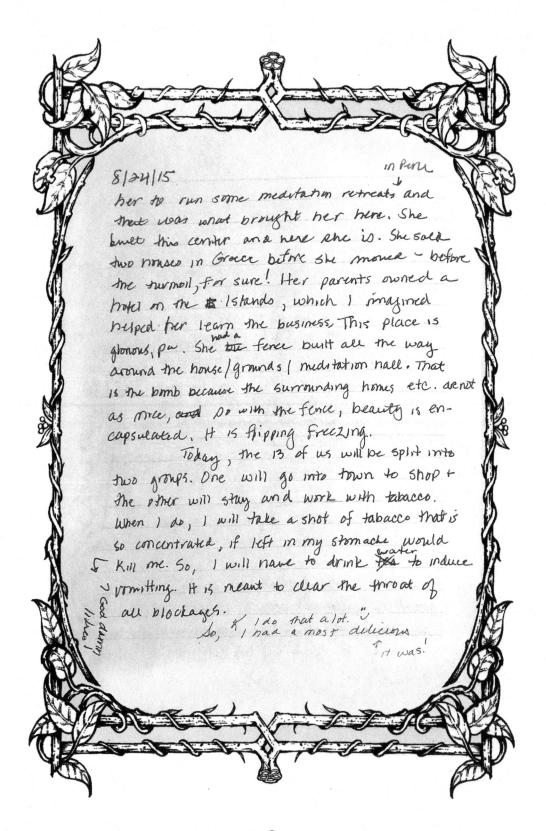

8/24/15

her to run some meditation retreats and ~~there~~ was ~~what~~ brought her here. She built this center and here she is. She sold two ~~houses~~ in Greece before she moved ~ before the turmoil, for sure! Her parents owned a hotel on the ~~▨~~ Islands, which I imagined helped her learn the business. This place is glorious, pw. She ~~had~~ ~~had a~~ ~~the~~ fence built all the way around the house/grounds/meditation hall. That is the bomb because the surrounding homes etc. are not as nice, ~~and~~ so with the fence, beauty is en-capsulated. It is flipping freezing.

Today, the 13 of us will be split into two groups. One will go into town to shop + the other will stay and work with tobacco. When I do, I will take a shot of tobacco that is so concentrated, if left in my stomache would kill me. So, I will have to drink ~~tea~~ water to induce vomitting. It is meant to clear the throat of all blockages.

So, I had a most delicious
↑ It was!

⌐ I do that a lot. ☺

God damn llamas

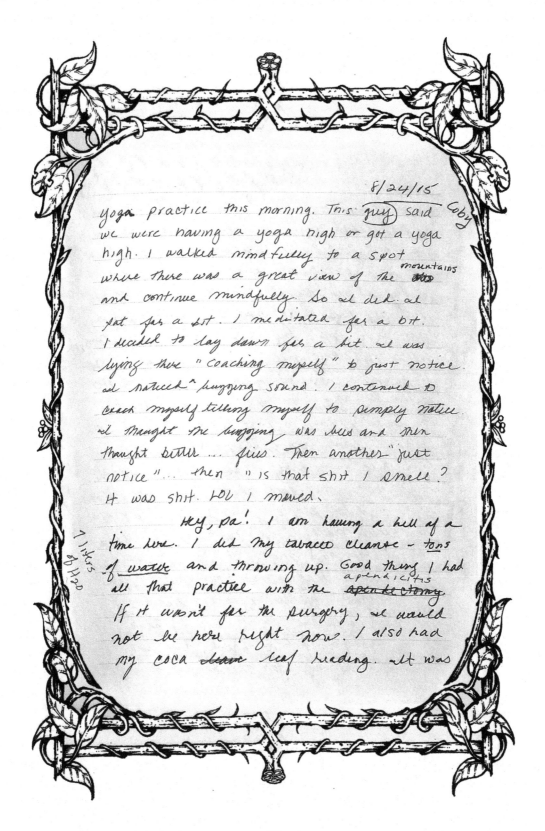

8/24/15

yoga practice this morning. This (guy) said Coby
we were having a yoga high or got a yoga
high. I walked mindfully to a spot
where there was a great view of the mountains
and continue mindfully. So I did. I
sat for a bit. I meditated for a bit.
I decided to lay down for a bit. I was
lying there "coaching myself" to just notice.
I noticed a buzzing sound. I continued to
coach myself telling myself to simply notice.
I thought the buzzing was bees and then
thought better ... flies. Then another "just
notice"... then "is that shit I smell?
It was shit. LOL I moved.

        Hey, pa! I am having a hell of a
time here. I did my tabacco cleanse - tons
of water and throwing up. Good thing I had
all that practice with the apendicitis
If it wasn't for the surgery, I would
not be here right now. I also had
my coca leaf reading. It was

7 liters
of H2O

29

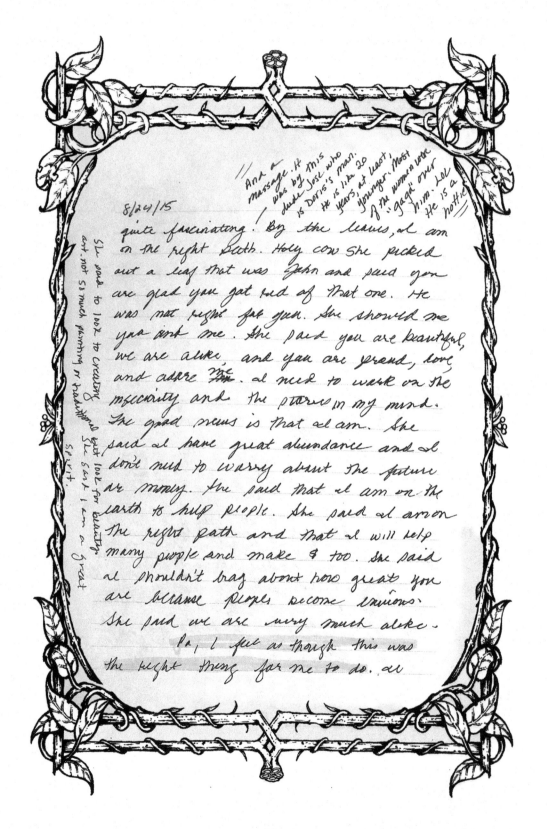

8/24/15

quite fascinating! By the leaves, I am on the right path. Holy cow she picked out a leaf that was John and said you are glad you got rid of that one. He was not right for you. She showed me you and me. She said you are beautiful, we are alike, and you are grand, love, and adore me. I need to work on the insecurity and the stories in my mind. The good news is that I am. She said I have great abundance and I don't need to worry about the future or money. She said that I am on the earth to help people. She said I am on the right path and that I will help many people and make $ too. She said I shouldn't brag about how great you are because people become envious. She said we are very much alike.

Pa, I feel as though this was the right thing for me to do. I

(top margin, written at angle) And a message. It was by this dude Jose who is Doris's man. He is like 20 years, at least, younger. Most of the women were "gaga" over him. LoL He is a hottie.

(left margin, written vertically) She said to look to creating art. not so much painting or traditional but look for beauty. She said I am a great spirit.

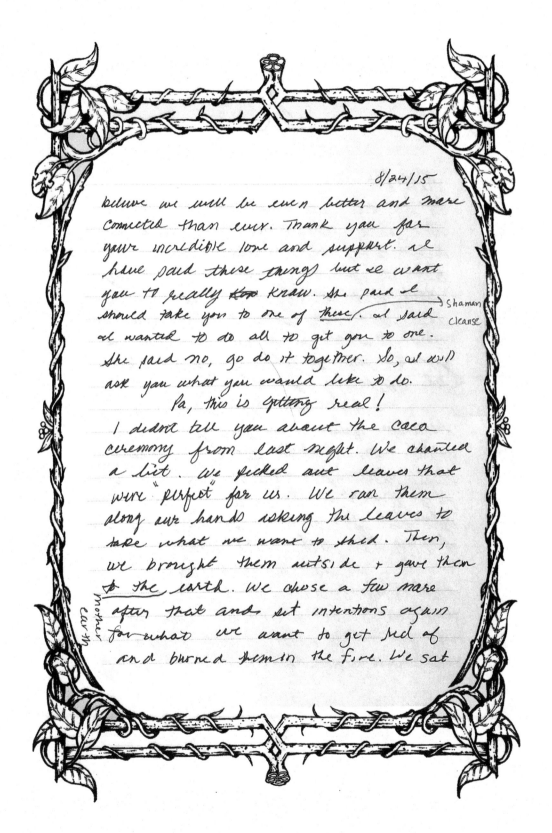

believe we will be even better and more
connected than ever. Thank you for
your incredible love and support. I
have said these things but I want
you to really know. She said I
should take you to one of these. I said →Shaman
I wanted to do all to get you to one.   cleanse
She said no, go do it together. So, I will
ask you what you would like to do.

Pa, this is getting real!
I didn't tell you about the coca
ceremony from last night. We chanted
a bit. We picked out leaves that
were "perfect" for us. We ran them
along our hands asking the leaves to
take what we want to shed. Then,
we brought them outside + gave them
to the earth. We chose a few more
             (mother
             earth)
after that ands set intentions again
for what we want to get rid of
and burned them in the fire. We sat

31

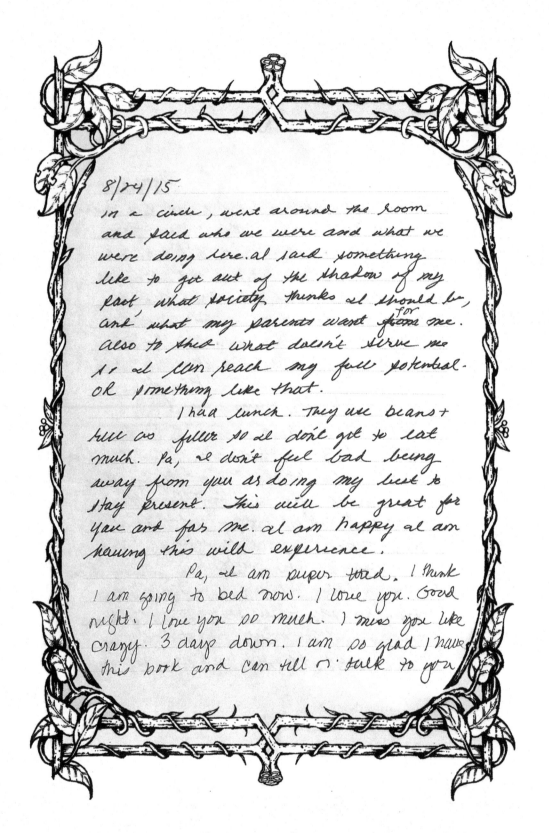

8/24/15

in a circle, went around the room
and said who we were and what we
were doing here. al said something
like to get out of the shadow of my
past, what society thinks al should be,
and what my parents want for me.
also to shed what doesn't serve me
so al can reach my full potential.
or something like that.

I had lunch. they use beans +
rice as filler so al don't get to eat
much. Pa, al don't feel bad being
away from you as doing my best to
stay present. this will be great for
you and for me. al am happy al am
having this wild experience.

Pa, al am super tired. I think
I am going to bed now. I love you. Good
night. I love you so much. I miss you like
crazy. 3 days down. I am so glad I have
this book and can tell or talk to you

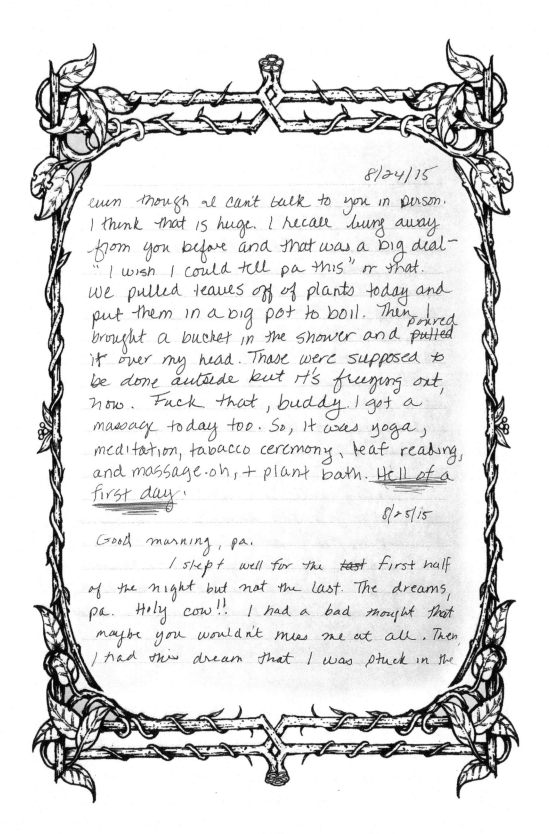

8/24/15

even though I can't talk to you in person.
I think that is huge. I recall being away
from you before and that was a big deal—
"I wish I could tell pa this" or that.
We pulled leaves off of plants today and
put them in a big pot to boil. Then I
brought a bucket in the shower and ~~pulled~~ poured
it over my head. Those were supposed to
be done outside but it's freezing out,
now. Fuck that, buddy. I got a
massage today too. So, it was yoga,
meditation, tabacco ceremony, leaf reading,
and massage. oh, + plant bath. Hell of a
first day.

8/25/15

Good morning, pa.

I slept well for the ~~last~~ first half
of the night but not the last. The dreams,
pa. Holy cow!! I had a bad thought that
maybe you wouldn't miss me at all. Then,
I had this dream that I was stuck in the

33

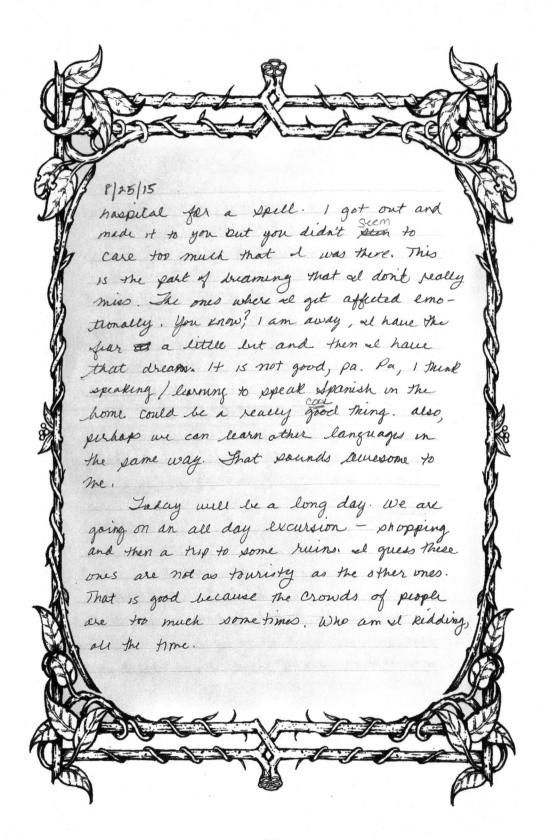

8/25/15

hospital for a spell. I got out and
made it to you but you didn't seem to
care too much that I was there. This
is the part of dreaming that I don't really
miss. The ones where I get affected emotionally. You know? I am away, I have the
fear a little bit and then I have
that dream. It is not good, pa. Pa, I think
speaking / learning to speak Spanish in the
home could be a really cool good thing. also,
perhaps we can learn other languages in
the same way. That sounds awesome to
me.

      Today will be a long day. We are
going on an all day excursion — shopping
and then a trip to some ruins. I guess these
ones are not as touristy as the other ones.
That is good because the crowds of people
are too much sometimes. Who am I kidding,
all the time.

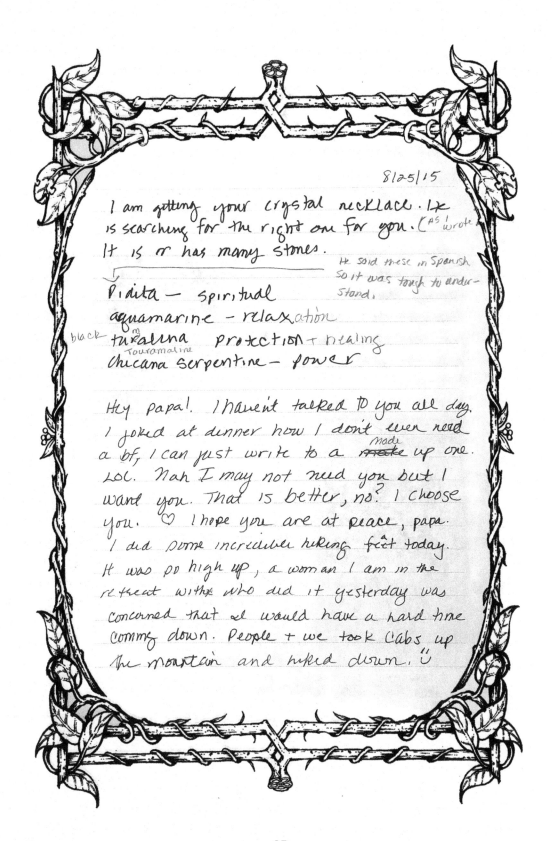

8/25/15

I am getting your crystal necklace. It is searching for the right one for you. (As I wrote) It is or has many stones.

_____

He said these in Spanish so it was tough to understand.

Piedita — spiritual
aquamarine — relaxation
black turalina protection + healing
Touramaline
Chicana serpentine — power

Hey papa! I haven't talked to you all day. I joked at dinner how I don't even need a bf, I can just write to a ~~make~~ made up one. LOL. Nah I may not need you but I want you. That is better, no? I choose you. ♡ I hope you are at peace, papa. I did some incredible hiking feet today. It was so high up, a woman I am in the retreat with who did it yesterday was concerned that I would have a hard time coming down. People + we took cabs up the mountain and hiked down. ☺

35

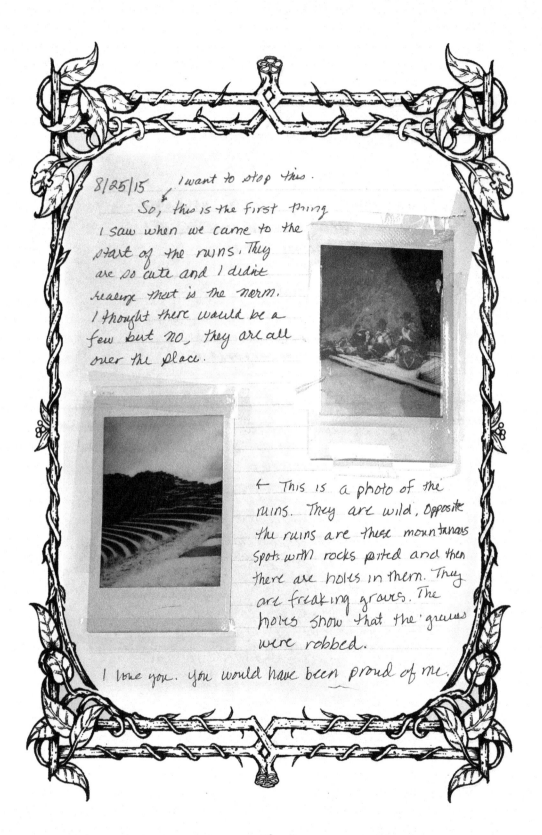

8/25/15 I want to stop this.

So, this is the first thing I saw when we came to the start of the ruins. They are so cute and I didn't realize that is the norm. I thought there would be a few but no, they are all over the place.

← This is a photo of the ruins. They are wild, Opposite the ruins are these mountainous spots with rocks parted and then there are holes in them. They are freaking graves. The holes show that the graves were robbed.

I love you. You would have been proud of me.

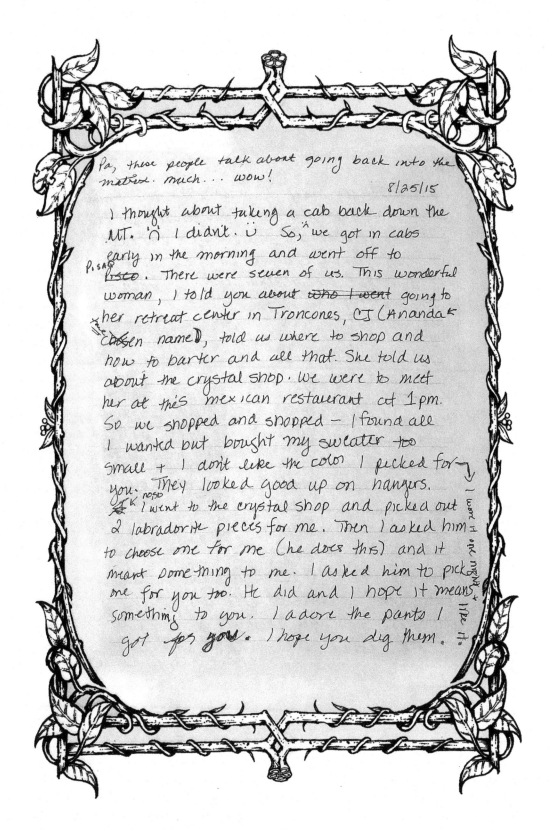

Pa, these people talk about going back into the
matrix much ... wow!

8/25/15

I thought about taking a cab back down the
Mt. 'n' I didn't. ☺ So, we got in cabs
early in the morning and went off to
~~Ixto~~. There were seven of us. This wonderful
woman, I told you ~~about who I went~~ going to
her retreat center in Troncones, CJ (Ananda
~~chosen~~ named), told us where to shop and
how to barter and all that. She told us
about the crystal shop. We were to meet
her at this mexican restaurant at 1pm.
So we shopped and shopped - I found all
I wanted but bought my sweater too
small + I don't like the color I picked for
you. They looked good up on hangers.
I went to the crystal shop and picked out
2 labradorite pieces for me. Then I asked him
to choose one for me (he does this) and it
meant something to me. I asked him to pick
one for you too. He did and I hope it means
something to you. I adore the pants I
got ~~for you~~. I hope you dig them.

8/25/15

We met for lunch — soup, stir fry, Peruvian mint tea, and plantains for dessert. What a perfect meal it was. Pa, I puked and they puked several times in front of one another — so we bonded. ü. Then, it was off to the ruins.

We rode up and got right to it. Pa, ~~the ruins~~ we kept climbing and climbing + climbing. It was nuts. I was "coaching" myself. I said at one point: Luke had to face his father Darth Vader, I can do this. AND I DID. It was cool. There was a high energy area — I felt the walls vibrating — subtly. This woman called ~~us~~ us over to this "room" she could feel energy. We all went in lock down and did ~~~~ some breathing

(I could or thought) felt something in my hands. ↓

8/25/15

and connected with the earth. We were laying on our backs and it was raining on us. What an incredible experience with all there was more bonding. It was super cool. No one is ever like, well that is weird. It is so cool and open. I am pooped after all this — we climbed down the mountain on trails. My knee (left) was dogged. Davis, the leaf reader said my knees are/will be trouble for me. It took awhile and there was a lone flute-like instrument playing for us and travelled down the Mt playing for us. that thing. We got to the bottom and went "home". I had an awesome dinner and chat. The other half of the group did their tabaceo ritual, so we caught up. Then it was time for song time.

One song was a Simon + Garfunkle song. →

Take a guess as to what that is... I am eating it, now. BITTER!!!!

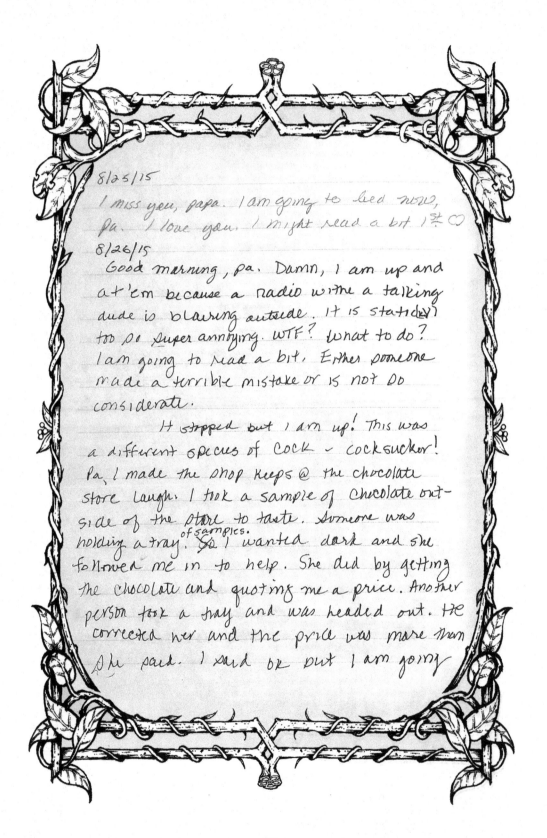

8/25/15

I miss you, papa. I am going to bed now, pa. I love you. I might read a bit 1st ♡

8/26/15

Good morning, pa. Damn, I am up and at 'em because a radio with a talking dude is blaring outside. It is staticky too so super annoying. WTF? What to do? I am going to read a bit. Either someone made a terrible mistake or is not so considerate.

It stopped but I am up! This was a different species of COCK – cocksucker! Pa, I made the shop keeps @ the chocolate store laugh. I took a sample of chocolate outside of the store to taste. Someone was holding a tray of samples. So I wanted dark and she followed me in to help. She did by getting the chocolate and quoting me a price. Another person took a tray and was headed out. He corrected her and the price was more than she said. I said ok but I am going

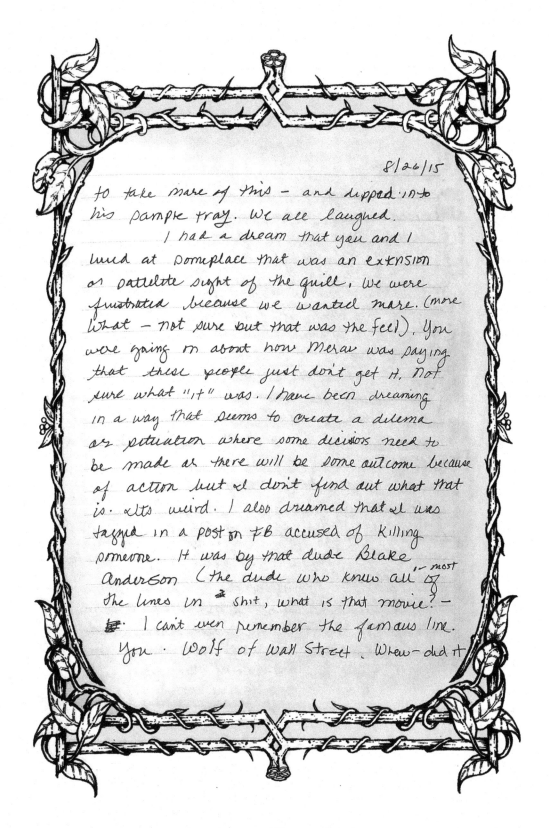

8/26/15

to take more of this — and dipped into
his sample tray. We all laughed.

I had a dream that you and I
lived at someplace that was an extension
or satellite sight of the quill. We were
frustrated because we wanted more. (more
what — not sure but that was the feel). You
were going on about how Merav was saying
that these people just don't get it. Not
sure what "it" was. I have been dreaming
in a way that seems to create a dilema
or situation where some decisions need to
be made as there will be some outcome because
of action but I don't find out what that
is. Its weird. I also dreamed that I was
tagged in a post on FB accused of killing
someone. It was by that dude Blake
Anderson (the dude who knew all ~ most of
the lines in shit, what is that movie? —
I can't even remember the famous line.
You · Wolf of Wall Street. Whew—did it

41

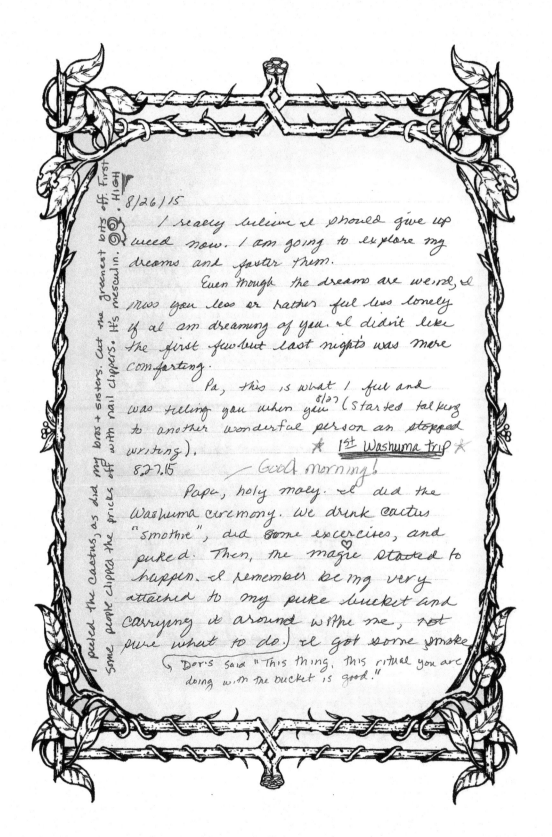

8/26/15

    I really believe I should give up weed now. I am going to explore my dreams and foster them.

    Even though the dreams are weird, I miss you less or rather feel less lonely if I am dreaming of you. I didn't like the first few but last nights was more comforting.

    Pa, this is what I feel and was telling you when you ⁸/²⁷ (started talking to another wonderful person an stopped writing).

    ★ 1st Washuma trip ★

8.27.15   — Good morning!

    Papa, holy moly. I did the Washuma ceremony. We drink cactus "smothie", did some excercises, and puked. Then, the magic started to happen. I remember being very attached to my puke bucket and carrying it around with me, not sure what to do.) I got some smoke

    ↳ Doris said "This thing, this ritual you are doing with the bucket is good."

(left margin, written vertically) I peeled the cactus, as did my bros + sisters. Cut the greenest bits off. First HIGH. Some people clipped the pricks off with nail clippers. It's mesculin.

42

Rapé
~~Rapay~~
(calms the mind, grounds, +
clears the path in nose)

ask more of them, like all of them.

8.27.15

thing blown up my nose. Hold on, after
I puked, I sat for a bit and looked
around. Everything seemed brighter, I
could see all the ants and flying bugs
more clearly. It was unbelievable. I
felt € "weird". I kept laughing and
laughing because I kept thinking of
you and "weird". Anyway, I didn't
really know what to do with myself,
so I hopped in the hammock. I
spent most of the day in the hammock.
It was glorious! Pa, I was seriously
"tripping balls". Washuma is out of this
world. I was laying there and so much
made sense. I realized everything is
perfect. It was a big revelation. ~~because~~
~~it~~ It is also what Saris (said like
Dorice) was telling me. There is nothing
wrong. Everything is right. It is. It is
the mind my mind that fills up
with views of non-perfection. I also

It showed me everything has its place and, it is perfect.

8/27/15

Let go of what is "supposed" to be.
It was freeing! And not going to lie, trippy.
I took to this woman, Bonita and checked
in with her now and again. I saw
a visual of what I thought was a good
representation of perfection so snapped
a photo and went to show Bonita. I

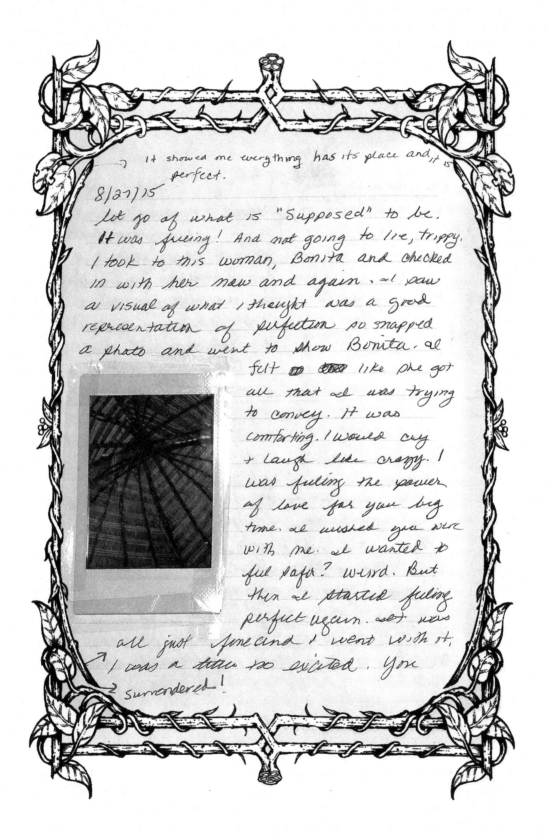

felt ~~so~~ ~~over~~ like she got
all that I was trying
to convey. It was
comforting. I would cry
+ laugh like crazy. I
was feeling the power
of love for you big
time. I wished you were
with me. I wanted to
feel safer? Weird. But
then I started feeling
perfect again. ~~It was~~

all just fine and I went with it.
I was a ~~little~~ so excited. You
surrendered!

know now I am. I continued to chill in
the hammock. I would collect things
and bring stuff to my cacoon. 😊.
I got out of the hammock and chilled
in the grass. People kept telling me
how great I looked. It had to be a rep.
of how I was feeling.
See →
We spent all day on
Washerma. It was a long
one. We were invited to
have a sound bath. We
went in to the temple
and ~~layed~~ laid on matts. It
was wonderful. ~~The~~ CJ's
friends came. 2 dudes
and a woman. One of
the dudes is from Australia or New Zealand.
CJ said he has like a 600 year old
soul. I was listening and then started
drumming with my hand on the carpet.

This woman Dawn said "Omie, how long have we been at this?" LULZ

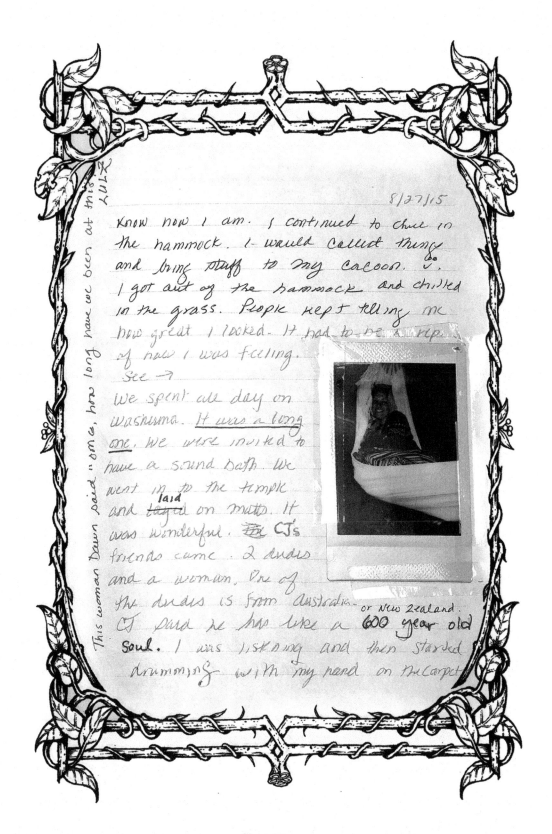

45

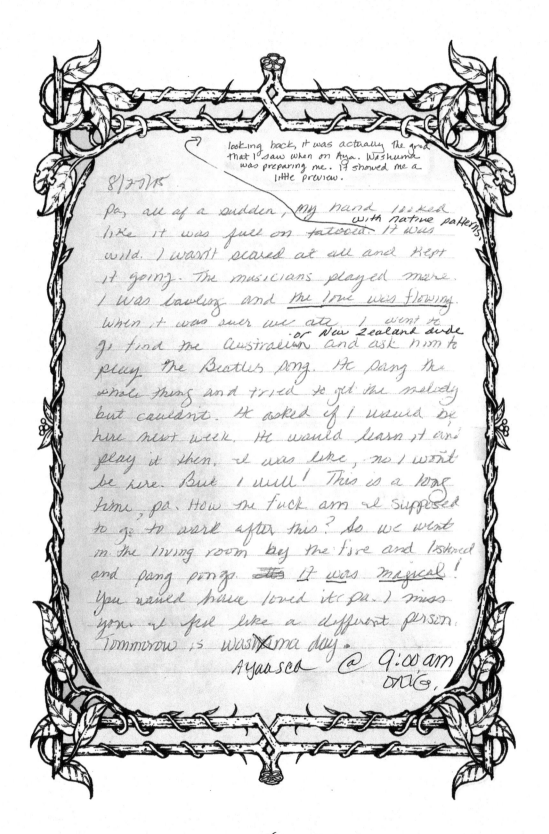

looking back, it was actually the guad
that I saw when on Aya. Washuma
was preparing me. It showed me a
little preview.

8/27/15

pa, all of a sudden, my hand looked
like it was full on ~~tatooed~~ with native patterns.
It was
wild. I wasn't scared at all and kept
it going. The musicians played more.
I was bawling and the love was flowing.
When it was over we ate. I went to
go find the Australian or New Zealand dude and ask him to
play the Beatles song. He sang the
whole thing and tried to get the melody
but couldn't. He asked if I would be
here next week. He would learn it and
play it then. I was like, no I won't
be here. But I will! This is a long
time, pa. How the fuck am I supposed
to go to work after this? So we went
in the living room by the fire and listened
and sang songs. ~~Its~~ It was magical!
You would have loved it pa. I miss
you. I feel like a different person.
Tommorow is washuma day.
           Ayaasca @ 9:00 am
                OMG.

46

8.27.15

we just came from an exhausting day in the town. We went shopping, to the Cacao Museum, more shopping, and then to lunch. Holy moly am I tired and fun. I sent you and your parents a postcard today. Pa, I dont want to do anymore promotion for the FSP or be in the writing club. It isn't my passion anymore.

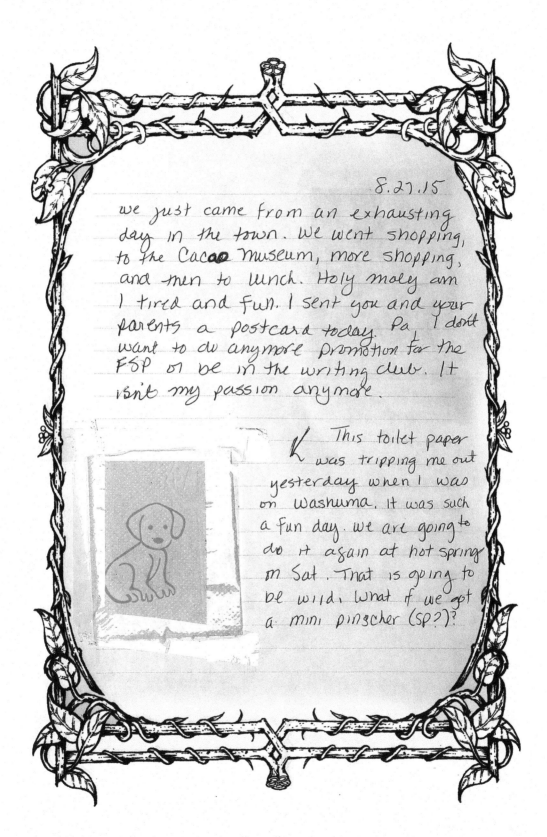

This toilet paper was tripping me out yesterday when I was on Washuma. It was such a fun day. We are going to do it again at hot spring on Sat. That is going to be wild. What if we got a mini pinscher (sp?)?

a workshop
at the cacoa museum

Replica of a
cocao tree @ the
museum.

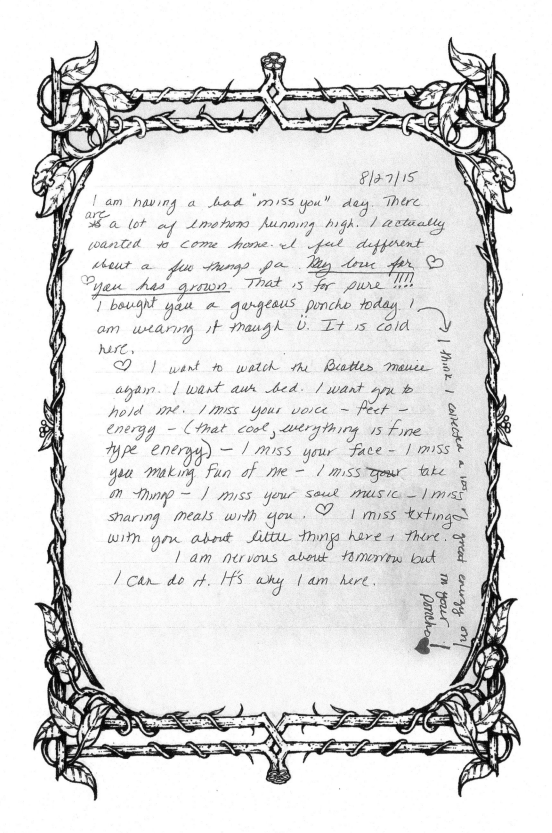

8/27/15

I am having a bad "miss you" day. There are a lot of emotions running high. I actually wanted to come home. I feel different about a few things pa. My love for you has grown. That is for sure !!!! I bought you a gorgeous poncho today. I am wearing it though ☺. It is cold here.

♡ I want to watch the Beatles movie again. I want our bed. I want you to hold me. I miss your voice — feet — energy — (that cool, everything is fine type energy) — I miss your face — I miss you making fun of me — I miss your take on things — I miss your soul music — I miss sharing meals with you. ♡ I miss texting with you about little things here + there.

I am nervous about tomorrow but I can do it. It's why I am here.

I think I collected a lot of great energy in your poncho!

49

8/27/15

Papa, I just took a plant bath outside, naked! It is almost a full moon. I was afraid to do it but then was going to have my new friend hold your poncho to cover me and do it. I decided to just do it and did. I did it quickly and it didn't seem ceremonial but rather quick. I was more focused on the naked part. I overcame a fear. That was cool. The water was warm and the plants smelled so nice.

Gift from shop keep.

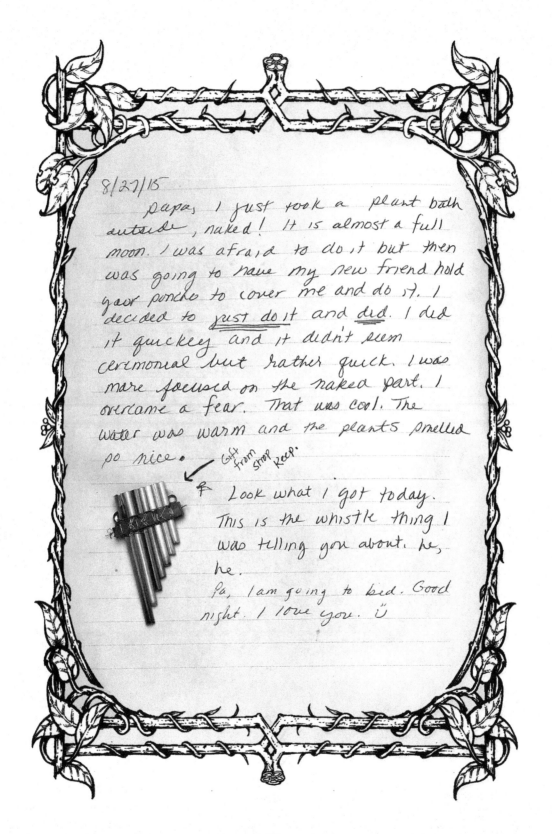

Look what I got today. This is the whistle thing I was telling you about. he, he.

Pa, I am going to bed. Good night. I love you. ☺

50

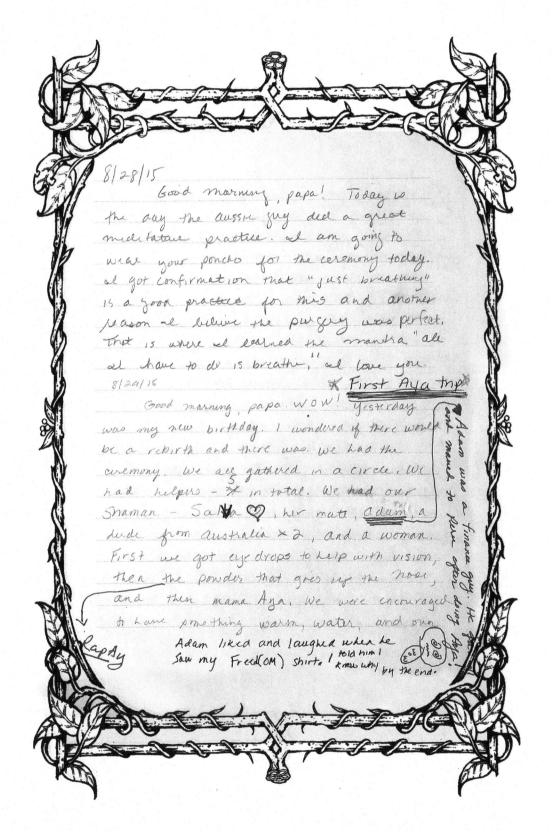

8/28/15

Good morning, papa! Today is the day the aussie guy did a great meditative practice. I am going to wear your poncho for the ceremony today. I got confirmation that "just breathing" is a good practice for this and another reason I believe the surgery was perfect. That is where I learned the mantra "all I have to do is breathe." I love you.

8/29/15   ✳ First Aya trip✳

Good morning, papa. WOW! Yesterday was my new birthday. I wondered if there would be a rebirth and there was. We had the ceremony. We all gathered in a circle. We had helpers - 5✳ in total. We had our Shaman - Salva ♡, her mate, Adam, a dude from Australia ✗2, and a woman. First we got eye drops to help with vision, then the powder that goes up the nose, and then mama Aya. We were encouraged to have something warm, water, and our

papAy

♥ Adam was a finance guy. He got out mad to live after doing Aya.

Adam liked and laughed when he saw my Freed(OM) shirt! I told him I knew why by the end.

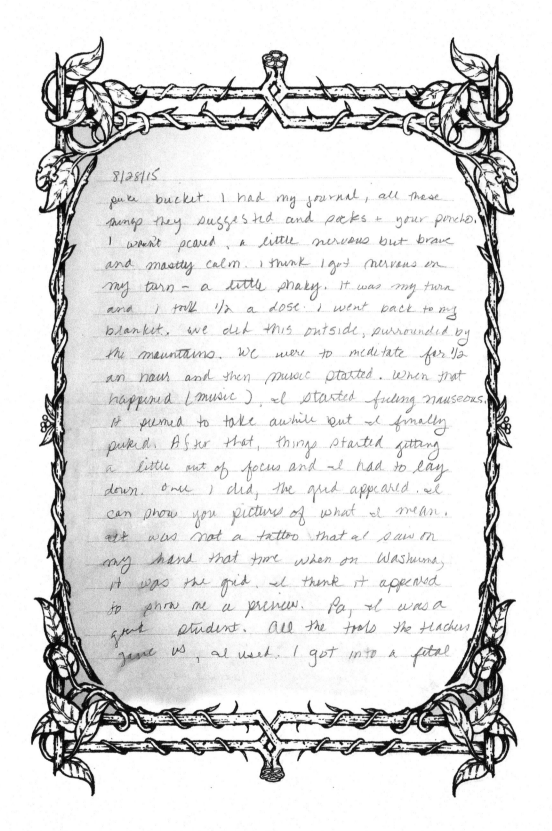

8/28/15

puke bucket. I had my journal, all these
things they suggested and socks + your poncho.
I wasn't scared, a little nervous but brave
and mostly calm. I think I got nervous on
my turn - a little shaky. It was my turn
and I took 1/2 a dose. I went back to my
blanket. We did this outside, surrounded by
the mountains. We were to meditate for 1/2
an hour and then music started. When that
happened (music), I started feeling nauseous.
It seemed to take awhile but I finally
puked. After that, things started getting
a little out of focus and I had to lay
down. Once I did, the grid appeared. I
can show you pictures of what I mean.
It was not a tattoo that I saw on
my hand that time when on Washuma,
it was the grid. I think it appeared
to show me a preview. Pa, I was a
great student. All the tools the teachers
gave us, I used. I got into a fetal

52

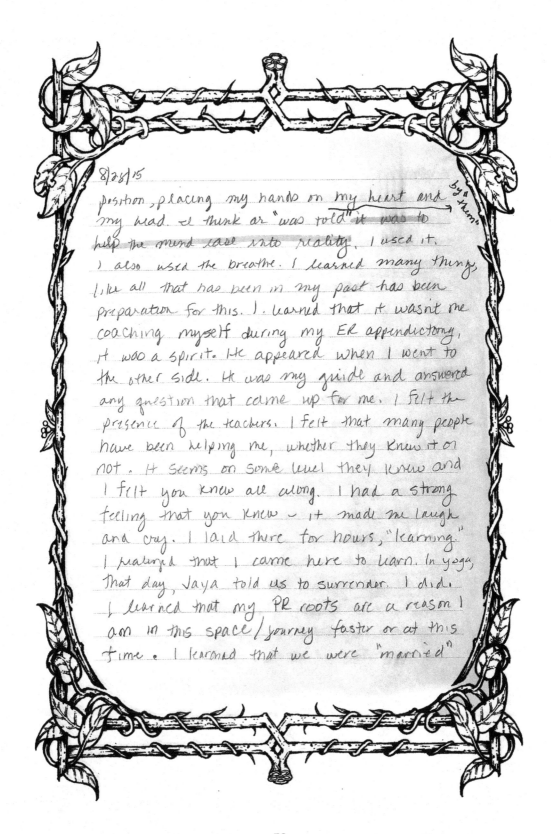

8/28/15

position, placing my hands on my heart and by "them" → my head. I think or "was told" it was to help the mind ease into reality. I used it. I also used the breathe. I learned many things, like all that has been in my past has been preparation for this. I learned that it wasn't me coaching myself during my ER appendictomy, it was a spirit. He appeared when I went to the other side. He was my guide and answered any question that came up for me. I felt the presence of the teachers. I felt that many people have been helping me, whether they knew it or not. It seems on some level they knew and I felt you knew all along. I had a strong feeling that you knew ~ it made me laugh and cry. I laid there for hours, "learning." I realized that I came here to learn. In yoga, that day, Jaya told us to surrender. I did. I learned that my PR roots are a reason I am in this space/journey faster or at this time. I learned that we were "married"

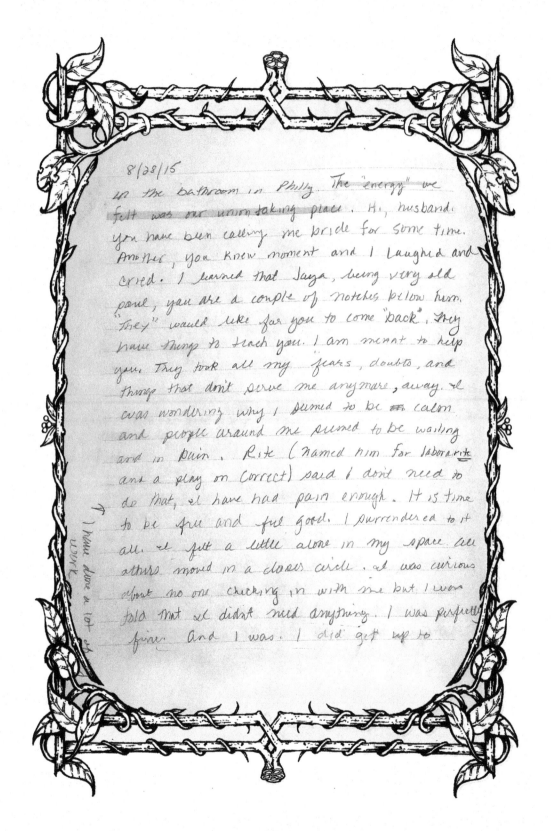

8/28/15

in the bathroom in Philly. The "energy" we ~~felt was our union taking place~~. Hi, husband. You have been calling me bride for some time. Another, you knew moment and I laughed and cried. I learned that Jaya, being very old soul, you are a couple of notches below him. "They" would like for you to come "back". They have things to teach you. I am meant to help you. They took all my "fears, doubts, and things that don't serve me anymore, away. I was wondering why I seemed to be so calm and people around me seemed to be wailing and in pain. Rite (named him for laborarite and a play on correct) said I don't need to do that, I have had pain enough. It is time to be free and feel good. I surrendered to it all. I felt a little alone in my space all others moved in a closer circle. I was curious about no one checking in with me but I was told that I didn't need anything. I was perfectly fine. And I was. I did get up to

↑ I have done a lot of work

54

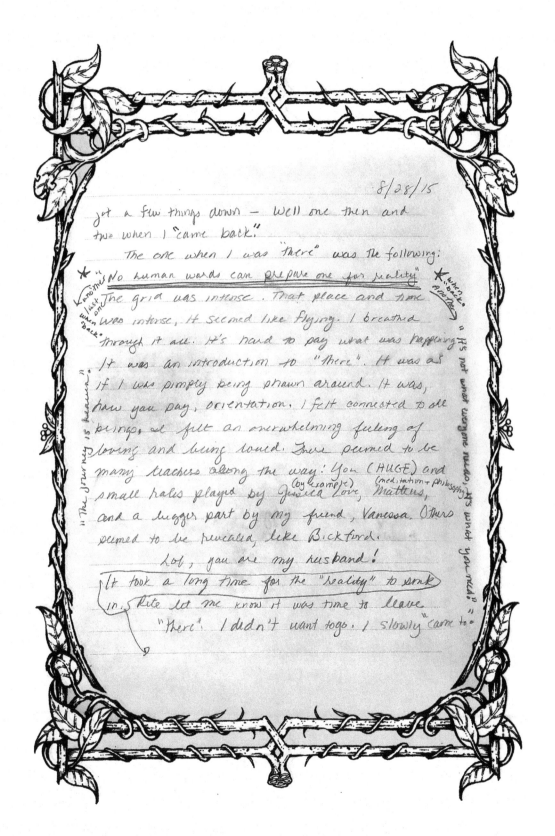

jot a few things down — Well one then and
two when I "came back."

The one when I was "there" was the following:

*"...me No human words can prepare one for reality" ← when "back"? another?

another last one The grid was intense. That place and now
when "back" was intense, It seemed like flying. I breathed
through it all. It's hard to say what was happening.
It was an introduction to "there". It was as
if I was simply being shown around. It was,
how you say, orientation. I felt connected to all
beings. I felt an overwhelming feeling of
loving and being loved. There seemed to be
many teachers along the way: You (HUGE) and
small roles played by Jessica Love, Matteus (by example), (meditation + philosophy)
and a bigger part by my friend, Vanessa. Others
seemed to be revealed, like Bickford.

"The journey is heaven."

"It's not what everyone needs, it's what you need!"

Lob, you are my husband!

It took a long time for the "reality" to sink
in, Kite let me know it was time to leave
"there". I didn't want to go. I slowly "came to."

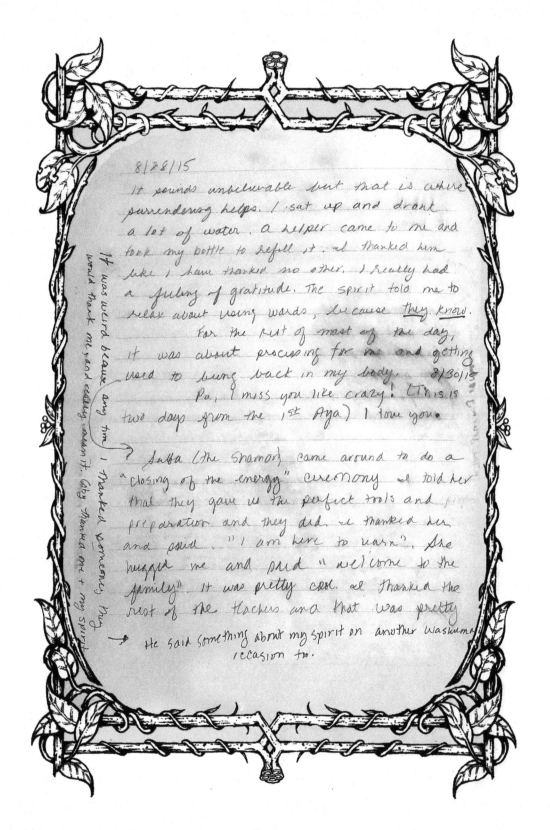

8/28/15

It sounds unbelievable but that is where surrendering helps. I sat up and drank a lot of water. A helper came to me and took my bottle to refill it. I thanked him like I have thanked no other. I really had a feeling of gratitude. The spirit told me to relax about using words, because <u>they know</u>.

For the rest of most of the day, it was about processing for me and getting used to being back in my body... 8/30/15

Pa, I miss you like crazy! (This is two days from the 1st Aya) I love you.

Saba (the shaman) came around to do a "closing of the energy" ceremony & told her that they gave us the perfect tools and preparation and they did. I thanked her and said, "I am here to learn". She hugged me and said "welcome to the family". It was pretty cool. I thanked the rest of the teachers and that was pretty

→ He said something about my spirit on another Wasuma occasion too.

It was weird because any time I thanked someones they would thank me and really mean it. Gaby thanked me + my spirit

56

much the day There may be more details but I am writing this a few days later, as I wrote.

Many people swapped the stories of their journey. Some were more intense than others. * 2nd Washuma trip *

The next day we boarded a bus (mercedes) headed for the hot springs for an overnight. We got to the place and the bus drove us to the most beautiful spot. We did going to do our 2nd Washuma ceremony here.

view from spot we did Washuma —

I did ½ a cup. I chilled there and then went down river to chill by myself. It was so beautiful and chill. I then started to fly high as a mother fucker. It was too intense for me. We started packing up and took the most

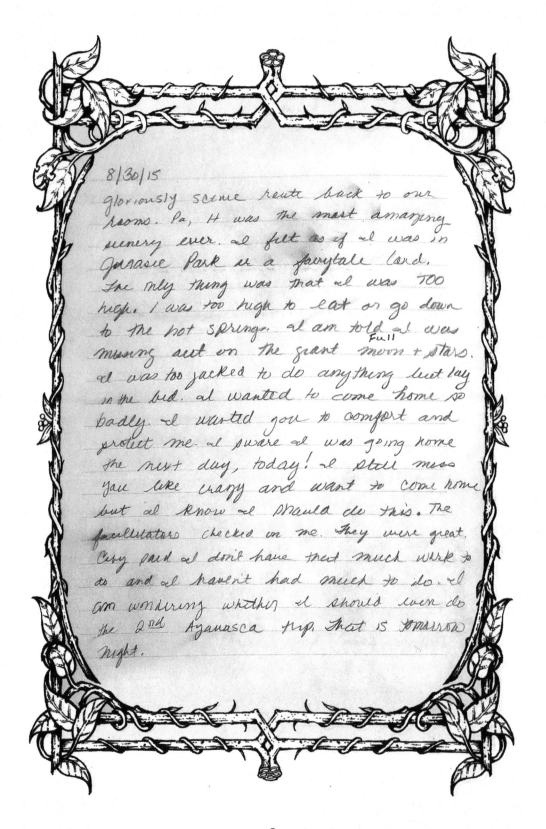

8/30/15

gloriously scenic route back to our rooms. Pa, it was the most amazing scenery ever. I felt as if I was in Jurassic Park or a fairytale land. The only thing was that I was TOO high. I was too high to eat or go down to the hot springs. I am told I was missing out on the giant Full moon + stars. I was too jacked to do anything but lay in the bed. I wanted to come home so badly. I wanted you to comfort and protect me. I swore I was going home the next day, today! I still miss you like crazy and want to come home but I know I should do this. The facilitators checked on me. They were great. Coby said I don't have that much work to do and I haven't had much to do. I am wondering whether I should even do the 2nd Ayanasca trip. That is tomorrow night.

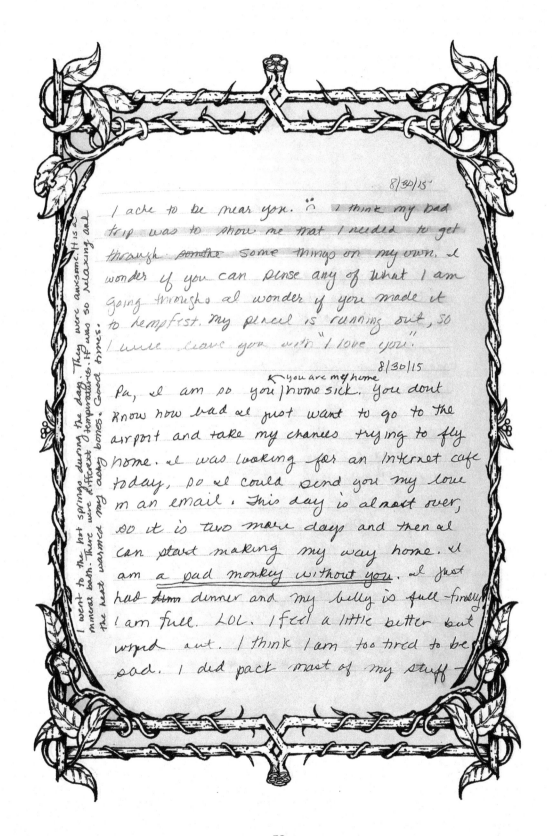

8/30/15

I ache to be near you. :) I think my bad trip was to show me that I needed to get through ~~somethe~~ some things on my own. I wonder if you can sense any of what I am going through. I wonder if you made it to hempfest. My pencil is running out, so I will leave you with "I love you".

8/30/15

Pa, I am so ~~you~~ |home sick. ↖ you are my home You don't know how bad I just want to go to the airport and take my chances trying to fly home. I was looking for an internet cafe today, so I could send you my love in an email. This day is almost over, so it is two more days and then I can start making my way home. I am a sad monkey without you. I just had ~~din~~ dinner and my belly is full—finally I am full. LOL. I feel a little better but wiped out. I think I am too tired to be sad. I did pack most of my stuff—

I went to the hot springs during the day. They were awesome. It is a mineral bath. There were different temperatures. It was so relaxing and the heat warmed my aching bones. Good times.

59

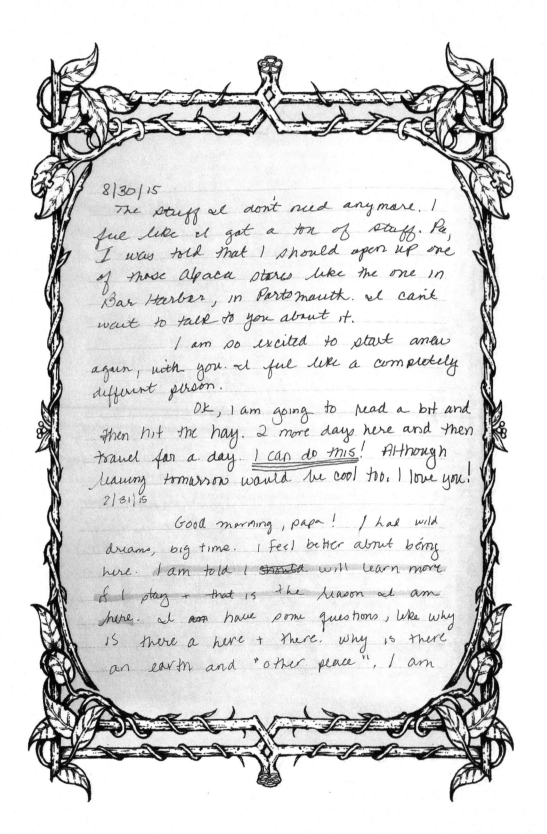

8/30/15

The stuff I don't need anymore. I feel like I got a ton of stuff. Pa, I was told that I should open up one of those Alpaca stores like the one in Bar Harbor, in Portsmouth. I can't wait to talk to you about it.

I am so excited to start anew again, with you. I feel like a completely different person.

Ok, I am going to read a bit and then hit the hay. 2 more days here and then travel for a day. <u>I can do this!</u> Although leaving tomorrow would be cool too. I love you!

2/31/15

Good morning, papa! I had wild dreams, big time. I feel better about being here. I am told I ~~should~~ will learn more if I stay + that is the reason I am here. I ~~am~~ have some questions, like why is there a here + there. why is there an earth and "other place", I am

60

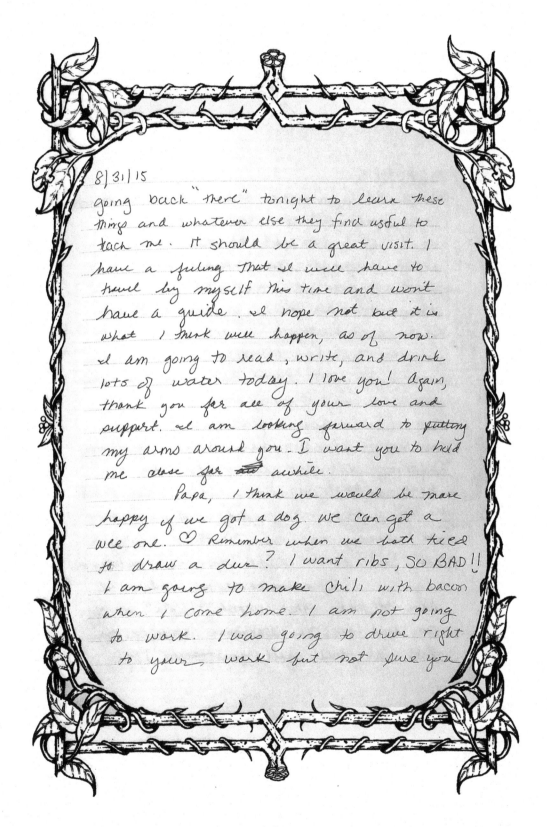

8/31/15

going back "there" tonight to learn these
things and whatever else they find useful to
teach me. It should be a great visit. I
have a feeling that I will have to
travel by myself this time and won't
have a guide. I hope not but it is
what I think will happen, as of now.
I am going to read, write, and drink
lots of water today. I love you! Again,
thank you for all of your love and
support. I am looking forward to putting
my arms around you. I want you to hold
me close for awhile.

        Papa, I think we would be more
happy if we got a dog. We can get a
wee one. ♡ Remember when we both tried
to draw a deer? I want ribs, SO BAD!!
I am going to make chili with bacon
when I come home. I am not going
to work. I was going to drive right
to your work but not sure you

61

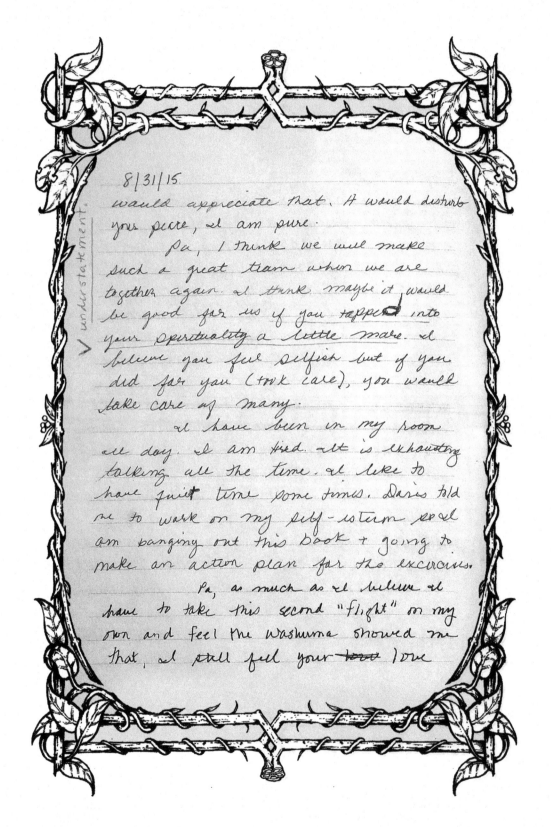

8/31/15.

would appreciate that. It would disturb your peace, I am sure.

Pa, I think we will make such a great team when we are together again. I think maybe it would be good for us if you tapped into your spirituality a little more. I believe you feel selfish but if you did for you (took care), you would take care of many.

I have been in my room all day. I am tired. It is exhausting talking all the time. I like to have quiet time some times. Daries told me to work on my self-esteem so I am banging out this book + going to make an action plan for the excercises.

Pa, as much as I believe I have to take this second "flight" on my own and feel the Washuma showed me that, I still feel your ~~true~~ love

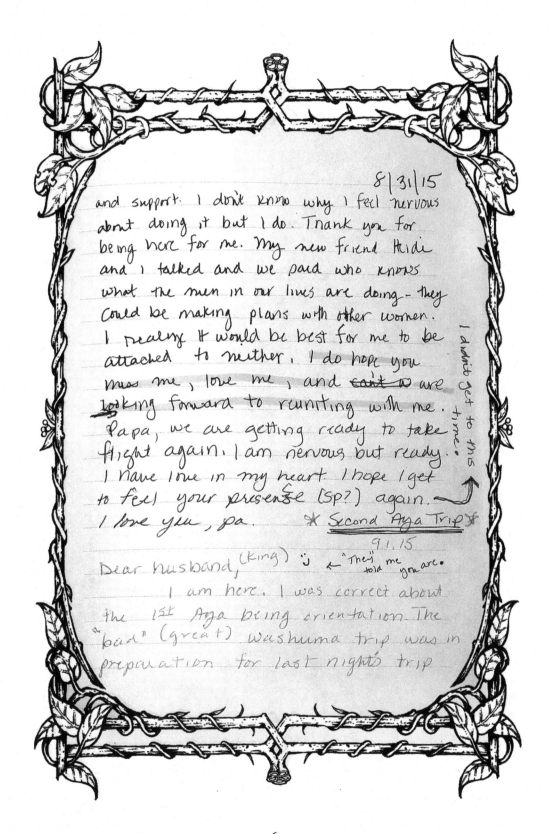

8/31/15

and support. I don't know why I feel nervous about doing it but I do. Thank you for being here for me. My new friend Heidi and I talked and we said who knows what the men in our lives are doing — they could be making plans with other women. I realize it would be best for me to be attached to neither. I do hope you miss me, love me, and ~~can't to~~ are looking forward to reuniting with me. Papa, we are getting ready to take flight again. I am nervous but ready. I have love in my heart. I hope I get to feel your presence (sp?) again. I love you, pa.   ✳ Second Aya Trip ✳

I didn't get to this time.

9.1.15

Dear husband, (king) :) ← "They" told me you are.

    I am here. I was correct about the 1st Aya being orientation. The "bad" (great) Washuma trip was in preparation for last night's trip

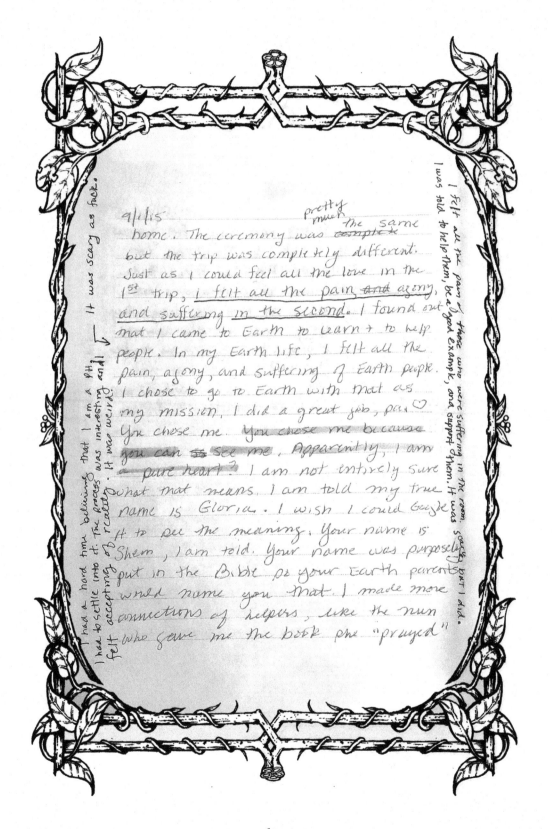

9/1/15

home. The ceremony was ~~complete~~ pretty much the same
but the trip was completely different.
Just as I could feel all the love in the
1st trip, I felt all the pain ~~and agony~~,
and suffering in the second. I found out
that I came to Earth to learn + to help
people. In my Earth life, I felt all the
pain, agony, and suffering of Earth people.
I chose to go to Earth with that as
my mission. I did a great job, pai ♡
You chose me. ~~You chose me because
you can see me.~~ Apparently, I am
~~a pure heart?~~ I am not entirely sure
what that means. I am told my true
name is Gloria. I wish I could Google
it to see the meaning. Your name is
Shem, I am told. Your name was purposely
put in the Bible so your Earth parents
would name you that. I made more
connections of helpers, like the nun
who gave me the book she "prayed"

I felt all the pain of those who were suffering in the room. I was told to help them, be a good example, and support them. It was scary but I did.

I had him believing that I am a PH! The process was interesting and I had to settle into it. It was weird. I felt accepting of reality.

It was scary as fuck.

64

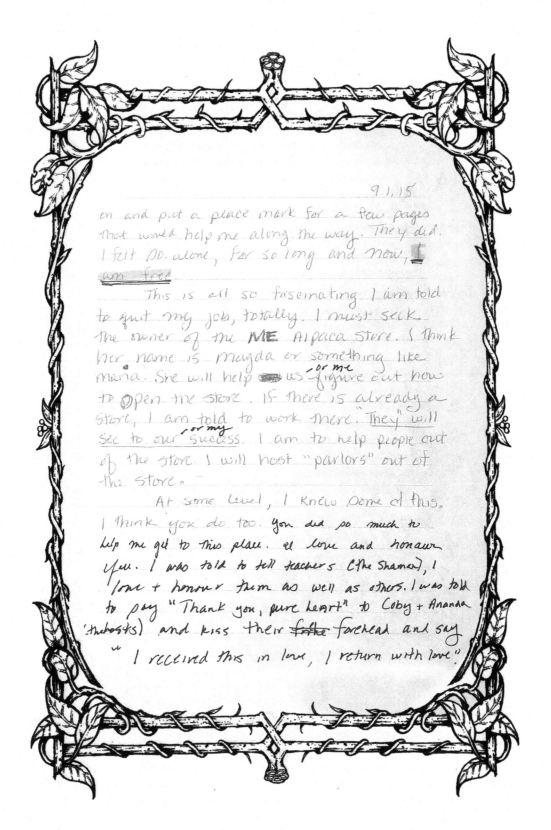

9.1.15

on and put a place mark for a few pages
that would help me along the way. They did.
I felt so alone, for so long and now, I
~~am free~~

This is all so fascinating. I am told
to quit my job, totally. I must seek
the owner of the ME Alpaca store. I think
her name is Magda or something like
maria. She will help ~~me~~ us -or me- figure out how
to Open the store. If there is already a
store, I am told to work there. "They" will
see to our -or my- success. I am to help people out
of the store. I will host "parlors" out of
the store.

At some level, I knew some of this.
I think you do too. You did so much to
help me get to this place. el love and honour
you. I was told to tell teachers (the shaman), I
love + honour them as well as others. I was told
to pay "Thank you, pure heart" to Coby + Ananda
(the hosts) and kiss their ~~for the~~ forehead and say
" I received this in love, I return with love."

9/11/15

Papa, music was a big part of the
healing. Jaya is the 600 year old guy. He is
so "the light".

The woman in the photo
is Marie, the owner
of the retreat center. She is
selling it and this guy. Luke
(a master in training) is going
to buy it. He came to the
Shamanic Cuame because
he saw his friend Bonita
post it on Facebook. When
Marie saw Luke, she
said he will be the one

to buy it. She knew. He said he
knew too. We drank Mama Aya at
night this time. We were all laid out
in the living room, COZY! It was totally
dark after the last person drank. They
waited 1/2 hour and then the music
started.

9/4/15

This other musician, Nacho played many instruments for us. They played the whole night, through. Here, he is playing the next day. They are gifted and giving. The music helps with the travel, big time!

Speaking of, we have the ~~2nd~~ runner up for Peru has got talent, playing at our party tonight. This will be a hell of a closing ceremony. I could listen to Jaya play all day long.

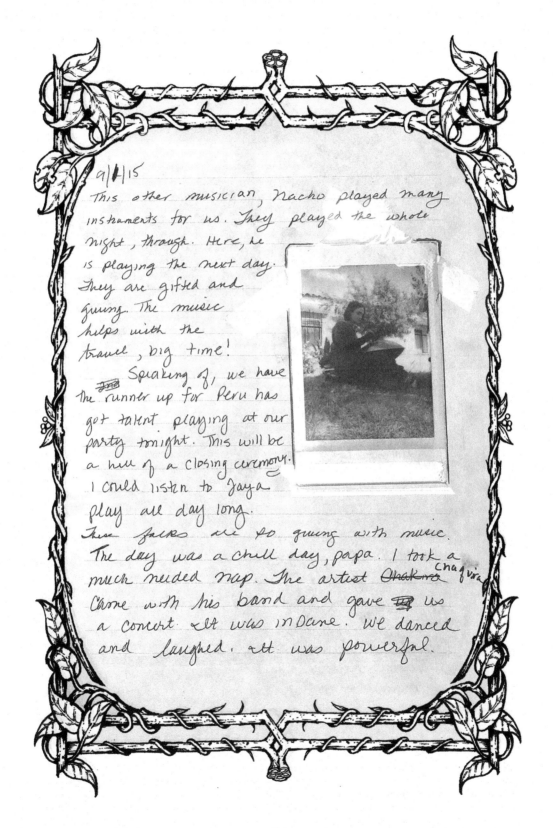

These folks are so giving with music. The day was a chill day, papa. I took a much needed nap. The artist ~~Chakura~~ Chaqira Corre with his band and gave ~~the~~ us a concert. It was insane. We danced and laughed. It was powerful.

9/7/15 They won 2nd in "Peru's got talent"

The concert →

not very good pictures.

Amaru, Album. Chaquira name.

Amaru, Pumac, Kuntur
Serpent, Puma, Condor (The Inca Trilogy represents balance!)

Her mom is
Doris (Dorice)
who "reads" coca
leaves. ♡

The shaman
Selva ~~selva~~ (Debora)

After the 1st Aya trip
I thanked her for the tools +
that I am here to
learn. She said "welcome
to the family" + gave me a
big hug.

I wrote this amigos

(Aussie dude)
Jaya aka Jesus to some
He never did
play the pong for me
but he did play me a
pong he wrote the morning
after Aya 2nd trip. It
was beautiful. + thanked ME
for listening to

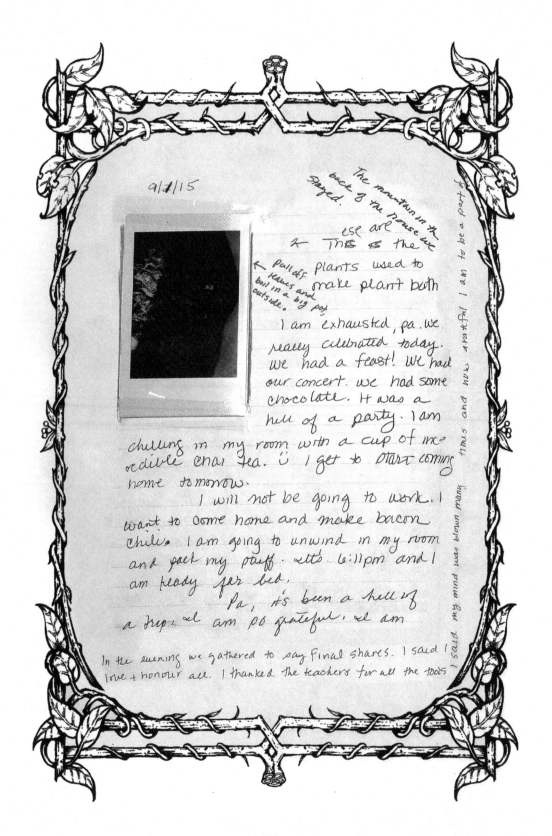

9/1/15

The mountain in the back & the house we stayed.

ese are ← This is the

← Pull off leaves and boil in a big pot outside. plants used to make plant bath

I am exhausted, pa. We really celebrated today. We had a feast! We had our concert. We had some chocolate. It was a hell of a party. I am chilling in my room with a cup of incredible chai tea. ☺ I get to start coming home tomorrow.

I will not be going to work. I want to come home and make bacon chili. I am going to unwind in my room and pack my stuff. It's 6:11pm and I am ready for bed.

Pa, it's been a hell of a trip. I am so grateful, I am

I am to be a part of times and was grateful I said my mind was blown many

In the evening we gathered to say final shares. I said I love + honour all. I thanked the teachers for all the tools

70

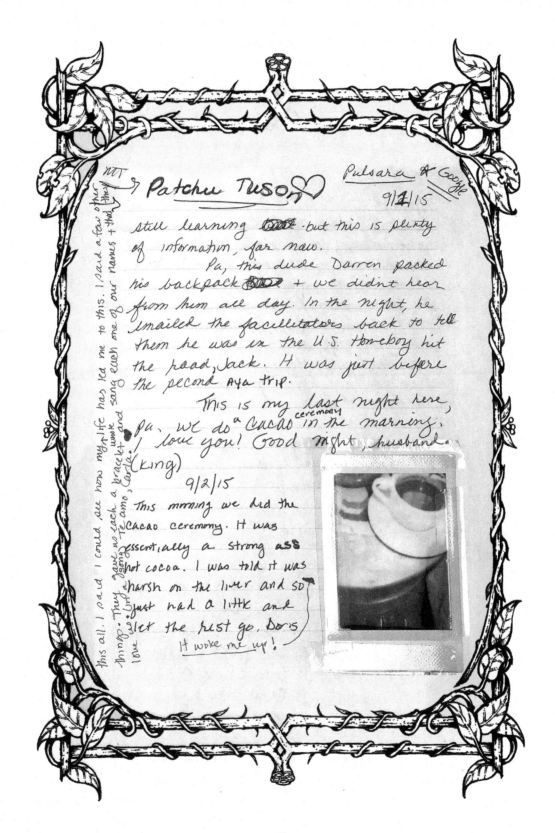

→ Patchu Tuson ♡

Pulsara & Google
9/1/15

NOT

still learning ~~stuff~~ but this is plenty
of information, for now.
        Pa, this dude Darren packed
his backpack ~~stuff~~ + we didn't hear
from him all day. In the night, he
emailed the facilitators back to tell
them he was in the U.S. Homeboy hit
the road, Jack. It was just before
the second Aya trip.
        This is my last night here,
Pa. We do a Cacao ^ceremony^ in the morning.
I love you! Good night, husband.
(King)
        9/2/15
This morning we did the
Cacao ceremony. It was
essentially a strong ass
hot cocoa. I was told it was
harsh on the liver and so
just had a little and
let the rest go. Dios
It woke me up!

(left margin, rotated): This all. I paid and I could see how my life has led me to this. I paid a few other things. They gave us each a bracelet and sang each one of our names + that they — Te amo, Carla. love you —

71

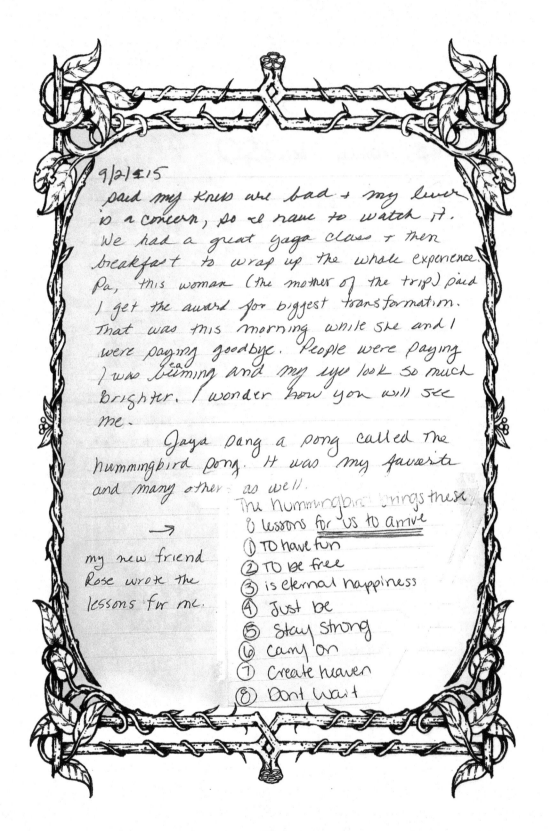

9/21≠15

said my knees are bad + my liver is a concern, so I have to watch it. We had a great yaga class + then breakfast to wrap up the whole experience. Pa, this woman (the mother of the trip) said I get the award for biggest transformation. That was this morning while she and I were saying goodbye. People were saying I was beaming and my eyes look so much brighter. I wonder how you will see me.

　　　Jaya sang a song called the hummingbird song. It was my favorite and many others as well.

my new friend Rose wrote the lessons for me. →

The hummingbird brings these 8 lessons for us to arrive
① To have fun
② To be free
③ is eternal happiness
④ Just be
⑤ Stay strong
⑥ Carry on
⑦ Create heaven
⑧ Don't wait

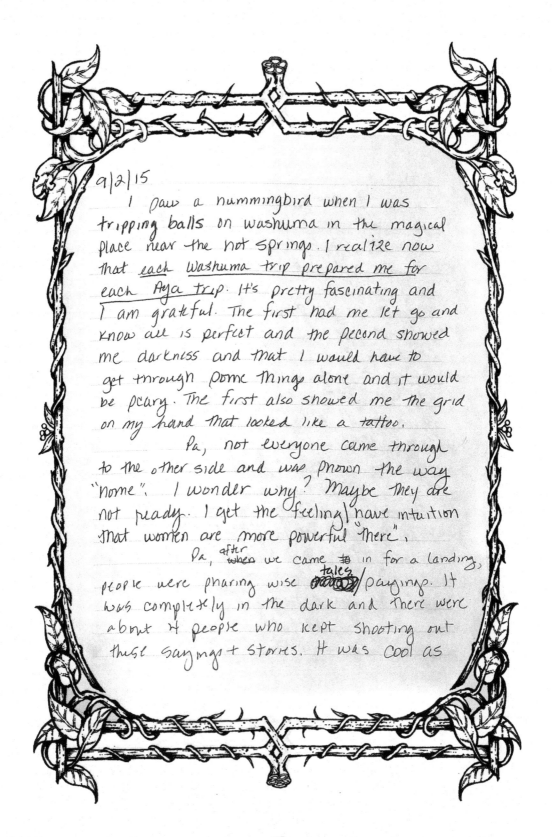

9/2/15

I saw a hummingbird when I was tripping balls on washuma in the magical place near the hot springs. I realize now that each Washuma trip prepared me for each Aya trip. It's pretty fascinating and I am grateful. The first had me let go and know all is perfect and the second showed me darkness and that I would have to get through some things alone and it would be scary. The first also showed me the grid on my hand that looked like a tattoo.

Pa, not everyone came through to the other side and was shown the way "home". I wonder why? Maybe they are not ready. I get the feeling/have intuition that women are more powerful "there".

Pa, after when we came to in for a landing, people were sharing wise ~~tales~~/sayings. It was completely in the dark and there were about 4 people who kept shooting out these sayings + stories. It was cool as

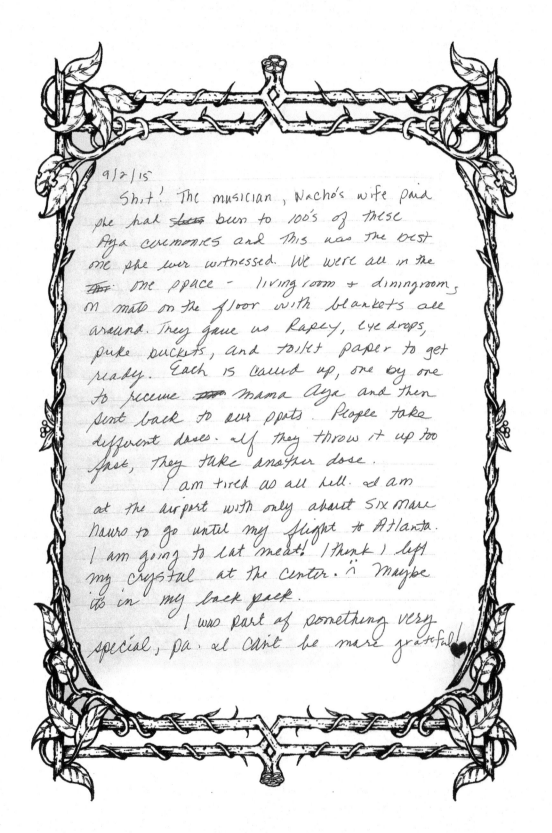

9/2/15

Shit! The musician, Nacho's wife said
she had been to 100's of these
Aya ceremonies and this was the best
one she ever witnessed. We were all in the
one space - living room + diningroom,
on mats on the floor with blankets all
around. They gave us Rapey, eye drops,
puke buckets, and toilet paper to get
ready. Each is called up, one by one
to receive mama Aya and then
sent back to our spots. People take
different doses. If they throw it up too
fast, they take another dose.

I am tired as all hell. I am
at the airport with only about six more
hours to go until my flight to Atlanta.
I am going to eat meat! I think I left
my crystal at the center. ⸚ Maybe
its in my back pack.

I was part of something very
special, pa. I can't be more grateful!

9/2/15

lol, you should see me. I look like a god damn hippy Peruvian chick. I feel great though. I have something called "Aqua florida". It is used to protect against bad energy (I think). I see some in the airport where luggage is checked. I hope they don't take mine. I also have washuma infused chocolates – got two out for this plane ride – lol. I hope I don't fly too high. I simply want to relax.

Pa, there are all kinds of plant medicine. (Mamapacha) means earth mother earth, to be specific. The symbol for her is something like:

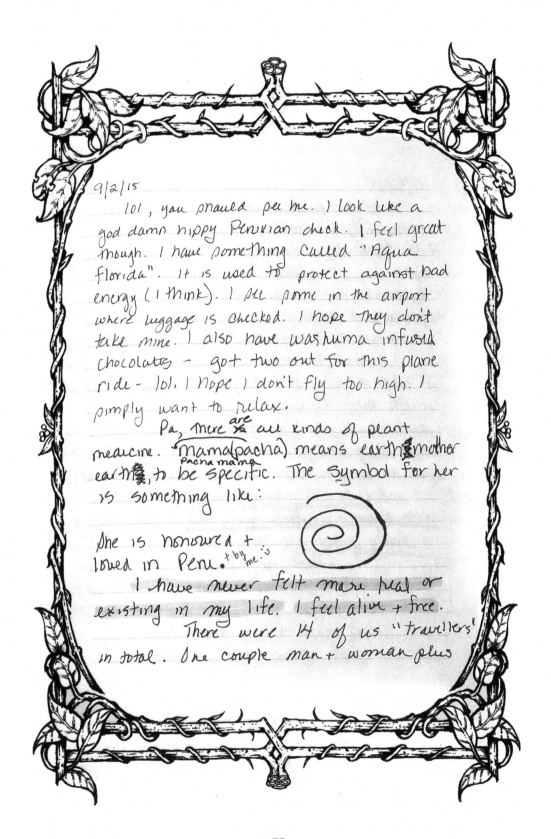

She is honoured + loved in Peru. + by me :)

I have never felt more real or existing in my life. I feel alive + free.
There were 14 of us "travellers" in total. One couple man + woman plus

75

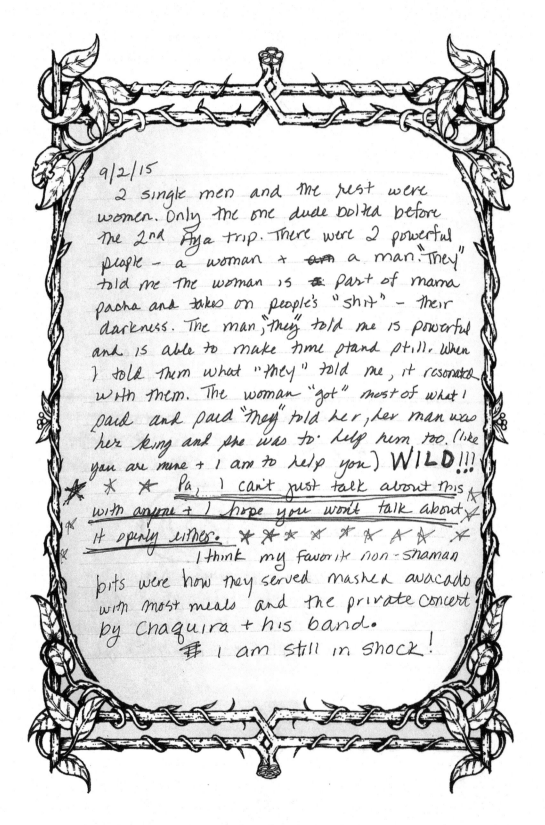

9/2/15
  2 single men and the rest were
women. Only the one dude bolted before
the 2nd Aya trip. There were 2 powerful
people - a woman + ~~an~~ a man. "They"
told me the woman is ~~t~~ part of mama
pacha and takes on people's "shit" - their
darkness. The man, "they" told me is powerful
and is able to make time stand still. When
I told them what "they" told me, it resonated
with them. The woman "got" most of what I
said and said "they" told her, her man was
her king and she was to help him too. (like
you are mine + I am to help you) WILD!!!
* * * Pa, I can't just talk about this
with anyone + I hope you won't talk about
it openly either. * * * * * * * * * *
       I think my favorite non-shaman
bits were how they served mashed avacado
with most meals and the private concert
by Chaquira + his band.
     ~~#~~ I am still in shock!

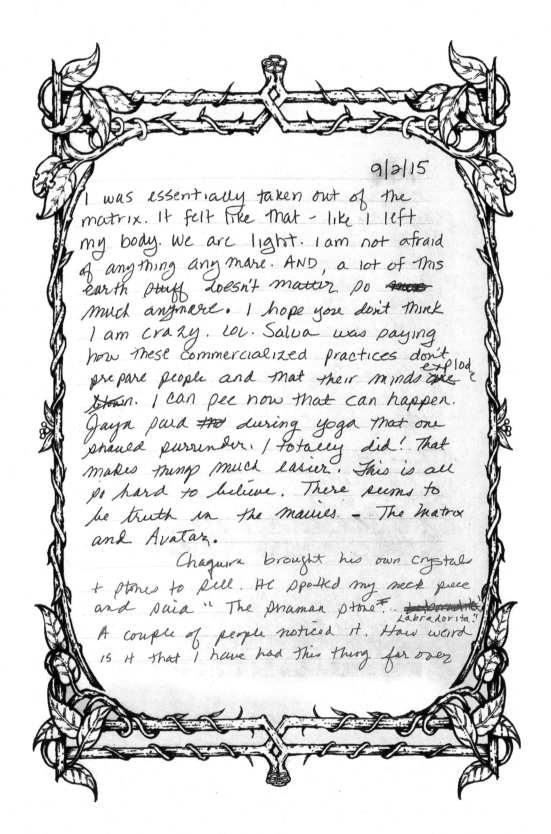

9/2/15

I was essentially taken out of the
matrix. It felt like that - like I left
my body. We are light. I am not afraid
of anything anymore. AND, a lot of this
earth stuff doesn't matter so ~~much~~
much anymore. I hope you don't think
I am crazy. lol. Salva was saying
how these commercialized practices don't
prepare people and that their minds ~~are~~ explode
~~blown~~. I can see now that can happen.
Jaya said ~~no~~ during yoga that one
should surrender. I totally did! That
makes things much easier. This is all
so hard to believe. There seems to
be truth in the movies. - The Matrix
and Avatar.

    Chaquira brought his own crystal
+ stones to sell. He spotted my neck piece
and said " The shaman stone ~~Labradorite~~
Labradorita."
A couple of people noticed it. How weird
is it that I have had this thing for over

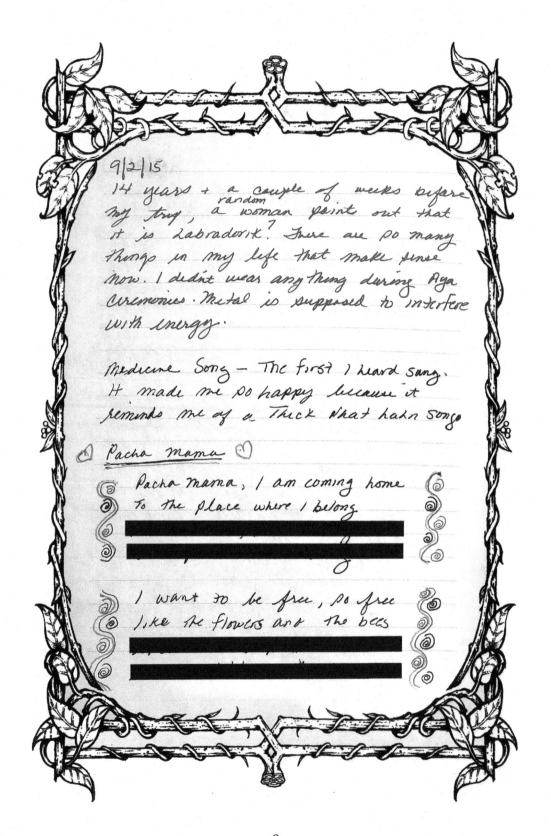

9/2/15

14 years + a couple of weeks before
my trip, a woman ^random point out that
it is Labradorik? There are so many
things in my life that make sense
now. I didn't wear anything during Aya
ceremonies. Metal is supposed to interfere
with energy.

Medicine Song — The first I heard sung.
It made me so happy because it
reminds me of a Thick Nhat hahn song

♡ Pacha Mama ♡

Pacha Mama, I am coming home
to the place where I belong

████████████████████████
████████████████████████

I want to be free, so free
like the flowers and the bees

████████████████████████
████████████████████████

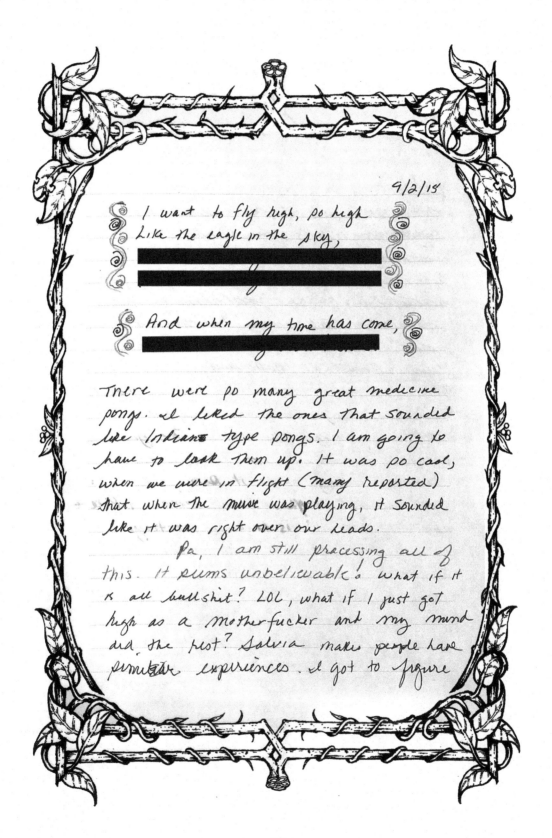

9/2/15

I want to fly high, so high
Like the eagle in the sky,
███████████████████████
███████████████████████

And when my time has come,
███████████████████████

There were so many great medicine
songs. I liked the ones that sounded
like Indian type songs. I am going to
have to look them up. It was so cool,
when we were in flight (many reported)
that when the music was playing, it sounded
like it was right over our heads.

Pa, I am still processing all of
this. It seems unbelievable! What if it
is all bullshit? LOL, what if I just got
high as a motherfucker and my mind
did the rest? Salvia makes people have
similar experiences. I got to figure

79

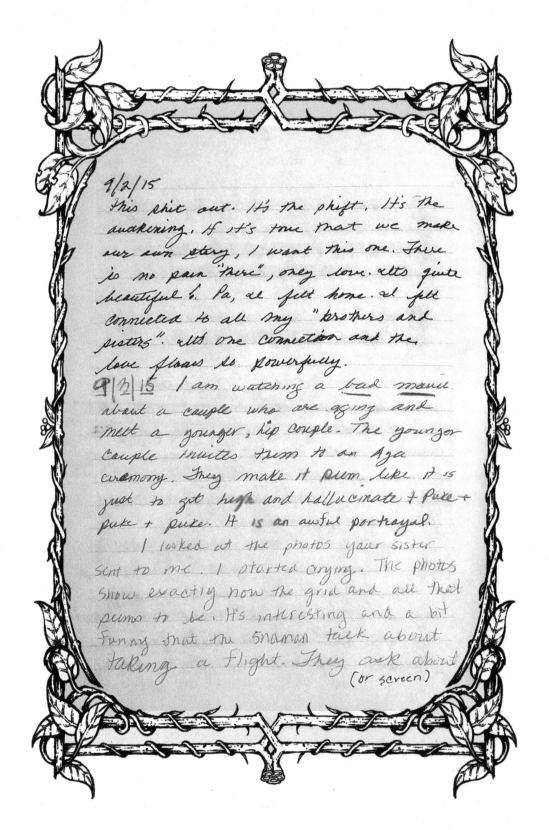

9/2/15
this shit out. It's the shift. It's the
awakening. If it's true that we make
our own story, I want this one. There
is no pain "here", only love. It's quite
beautiful b. Pa, I felt home. I felt
connected to all my "brothers and
sisters". It's one connection and the
love flows so powerfully.

9/3/15 I am watching a bad movie
about a couple who are aging and
meet a younger, hip couple. The younger
couple invites them to an Aya
ceremony. They make it seem like it is
just to get high and hallucinate + puke +
puke + puke. It is an awful portrayal.

     I looked at the photos your sister
sent to me. I started crying. The photos
show exactly how the grid and all that
seems to be. It's interesting and a bit
funny that the shaman talk about
taking a flight. They ask about
                              (or screen)

80

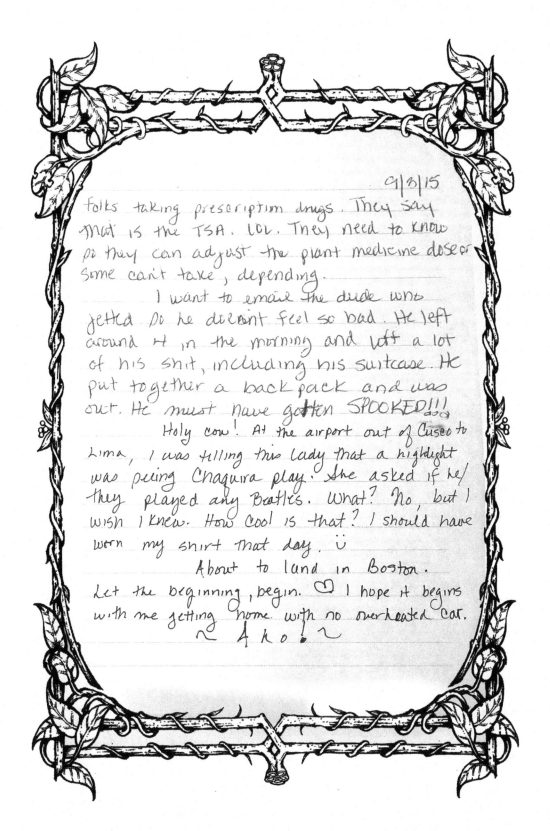

9/3/15

folks taking prescription drugs. They say
that is the TSA. LOL. They need to know
so they can adjust the plant medicine dose or
some can't take, depending.

    I want to email the dude who
jetted so he doesn't feel so bad. He left
around 4 in the morning and left a lot
of his shit, including his suitcase. He
put together a backpack and was
out. He must have gotten SPOOKED!!!

    Holy cow! At the airport out of Cusco to
Lima, I was telling this lady that a highlight
was seeing Chaquira play. She asked if he/
they played any Beatles. What? No, but I
wish I knew. How cool is that? I should have
worn my shirt that day. ☺

    About to land in Boston.
Let the beginning, begin. ♡ I hope it begins
with me getting home with no overheated car.
~ Aho! ~

Transcript/Notes

<u>Transcript</u> -

8.21.2015

I love you, pa! This is the first entry in my book to you. Ha, very exciting. (for me, anyway) I am on the plane to Atlanta. Plane (looks funny) There was a weird "gas" [a better word would be fuel] type smell I smelled when we first took off. I was scared. I thought, if I die, that is what I do next. It calmed me down. What can you do? Indeed!

I picked up this journal to write the following (but wound up writing the above too). I am reading 6 Pillars of Self-Esteem. I read the following. "We are not likely to see passionate romance between intelligence and stupidity" What does this remind you of right now? It was a romantic match I tried to make in my head. Going to go back to reading. This headache is starting up again. Booooo! I am still on the plane to Atlanta. OMFG - Just started to be turbulent. I wanted to thank you. While I didn't need your approval to go on this trip, I got it

Notes -

"What can you do?" is an expression I often say. Pa poked fun at me for this, among other things, by repeating this phrase in a thick, exaggerated Boston accent. I made it a habit of making fun of him, making fun of me. What could I do?

Since I was in a happy relationship with Pa, I wanted all those we cared about to be in one, too. I played matchmaker at times, especially in my head. I suggested aloud one match between two people who were on completely different intellectual levels.

I knew how absurd it was, once the thought left my lips, but Pa never let me live it down.

Page 2:

Transcript -
8.21.15
along with major support. That means a lot to me.

LOL. You should see my tray table - two journals, 2 pens, a highlighter, a book about photography and the Six Pillars of Self Esteem. At least no more turbulence. I may live!

Pa, remember I told you I was sad for my distant friend Yuki, who lost her baby boy before she could give birth? She delivered a healthy baby boy last week. When she was in labor, she asked her husband to play music and asked the nurse if it would be ok for her to dance. It was ok, so she did. He put on "Let me see you (or your) Tootsie Roll." She danced to that song, her water broke, and she was dilated a bit more. Her husband recorded it, it became an Internet sensation, and was played on local news stations. That is Yuki pa.

Notes
I am friends with Yuki on Facebook. I sure wanted to connect with her because she made such an impression on me when we were together in person at a club for dinner. Because of this video, she and her husband were invited on *The Ellen Show*, where they were given a car and car seat. It couldn't have happened to a nicer couple. I am attracted to unusual names, and her name is unusual, along with the name of her husband (Connell), daughter (Yume), and son (Cogi). Their angel son is named Yugi. They are a beautiful family, who make me happy to know of them.

Page 3:

Transcript -
8.21.15
I fell for her when I met her at the "dinner meetup". What a bright and beautiful woman. Natural Birth!!!

8.21.15
From HotLanta Flamage (Say like stoney)

I was lost and heard this woman say "Delta" to another lost person. I stood by to wait for her to help me, since I too, was looking for Delta. She looked at my ticket and said she wanted to come with me. She helped me and I mindfully looked into her eyes, thanked her, and told her to have a great day. Wait for it: She put both her hands to her heart and made a "bowing" motion. It moved me, I got chills, and teared up.

People down Southe no e are friendly (ier)
Friendlier than Boston
Warmer than NH folk

Do you like this style of communication? It is one way.

Notes
"Stoney" is a reference from the movie *Encino Man*. Pa and I found it funny that this is one of our favorite movies. I learned that he and his sister watched it a lot as young ones; it was one of my favorite stoner movies. On Earth, Pa and I were eleven years apart in age.

There is a kinder way to make note of differences about people I come across. Forgive my ignorance. I don't like generalizations. People are all different and complex. I don't know the full extent of myself. How am I to view these complex beings simply?

Page 4:

Transcript -
8.21.15
My brother Carlos Mora [who barely speaks to me.] posted a message on my post about going to Peru. I haven't written out my clear intention yet, pa.

Some of my thinking causes me to bust out with a Beatles tune.

Help … I need somebody …

… get by with a little help from my friends …

They just called over the loud speaker x Kobayashi. Do you know that name from the big screen?

6 hours 10 minutes.

On board! This chick (as you would say) spilled her H2O all over. She tried to store it overhead. So, the seat that got soaked, next to me, is EMPTY! Let me see your TOOTSIE ROLL. The flight attendant just gave us all earphones, earplugs, and a black

Notes
The facilitators supplied a preparation list for the shamanic cleanse, which included things to do and to avoid. Pa sent me a similar list he found online. One of the things suggested on the sheet he sent was to set an intention for meeting Mother Ayahuasca.

Pa and I watched a long documentary about the Beatles before I left for my trip. It took us about a week, with work and other obligations, to watch the whole thing, so the songs were stuck in my head.

We are big *Star Trek* fans. When Pa was young, he watched *The Next Generation* on television with his dad. They are such big fans; he and his family named their dogs Crusher and Data. He introduced me to the show by rewatching most of the episodes with me.

Page 5:

Transcript -
8.21.15
mask in the shape of a maxi pad, for our eyes. We got a blanket + pillow too. Pa, I am so happy I don't have to ask someone to move to go pee pee. You know me. [Rhymes Busta Rhymes was jailed recently.] I met this chick who saw me writing in my journal and said I inspired her to journal. I told her about the journal I am writing to you. She thought it was nice. I agreed and said I am not sure he will think so, since it seems he only listens to half of what I say - reading it all may bore him. he he You bored, pa?

I have written more in your journal than I have in me own. So yeah, six fucking hours and 10 minutes. Water is dripping on me. Dang, not sure if I should move my seat or stay. May not get easy bathroom access like I have now - pretty sweet. Ok I have to get to my journal + my intention.

Notes

It always surprised me what Pa would hear and what he wouldn't. He had a very scientific mind, so just the facts mattered to him (mostly). I am more wordy, adding details that could be left out and tell just as good of a story. I tried to be mindful of that in writing the side *Notes*
of this book.

Page 6:

Transcript -
8.21.15
They just came around with hot towels for our faces. We are all in first class, here on Delta.

We are about 1/2 way done with the flight. I am tired. I have a strong desire to get home and be in bed and near you. I miss you. I am trying to be here, in this moment but I keep thinking 2 weeks. It took a little longer when I went to Costa Rica, but I am thinking - why did you do it? Why did you put yourself in a position to be this uncomfortable? We both know why this time. We will be ok. This is not permanent. I love you.

The customs forms require me to put hotel info. I don't have one, lol. And, I don't recall the name of the place I am staying. Yowza! I hope they don't detain me.

I have a confession: Ready?

Notes -

It was always uncomfortable being away from Pa. I asked him if he would like to join me on a relaxing trip to Costa Rica (or anywhere). He replied that he didn't like the beach and didn't know how to relax. I went alone, and it was *extremely* awful without him, so I said I didn't ever want to do that again. When I wrote that "it took a little longer when I went to Costa Rica," I meant a little longer to realize I would have been happier at home with him.

8.21.15
I was on the verge of asking you if we could get a dog. It would have to be a little dog - that is the kicker and why I never asked. We can't have a dog - yet.

8.22.15

Pa Pa, I am in Lima, Peru. It's just after 1:00am and I am chilling (literally, cause these tiles are cold) on the floor at the airport. I am reading the complicated book on photography. I must be patient because there is much to learn. It can be overwhelming, esp. with all of these new (to me) terms. I am a little lonely. Some people who are on the floor are cuddled up with one another. I told you, you are like home, so I would feel so much better @ home. If you were here - in case you didn't get that. There are many other lone travelers, like me. Some of these people look like they are pure indigenous Andean. I may have made this up. I mean the wording. he he

Notes -
It's wild that I wanted a dog before I saw all of the awesome, free-roaming dogs in Peru. Seeing them must have put me over the edge.

There was a long layover at the Lima airport. I think many people got a hotel, but I winged it, along with others who lined the floor of the hallway we were in.

Page 8:

8.22.15
This chick who spilled the water just walked by, filming. I regret not giving her a little wave to the camera. I am letting it go. My bum is sore right about now. I have my hempies hat and my hippy bag - both items you bought for me. They afford a bit of comfort for me.

Pa, maybe this is like another rebirth for me. I know giving up the drink was. I am proud of us.

Mary Shell Story: I on FB a "summit" in Dedham, MA for alternative schooling. It was Thurs night. Mary Shell went and said she pulled her daughter our of school for this coming year. She said her daughter went-to 0% anxiety after and that she met other children that "get her". I posted about it, no specifics. I wrote that my friend's daughter is now at peace, the family is more at peace, and the world becomes more peaceful. I also wrote, I think this is how it (peaceful world) happens, on person at a time. Facebook isn't a complete waste. She thanked me + I told her she has the courage to try different things.

Notes -
"Hempies hat" refers to the hat he bought me, which is made out of hemp. Hemp is a great material that can make, among many other things, fabrics and building materials, and it can even replace plastic bottles, for those who may not know.

Pa and I gave up drinking alcohol about a year before I went to Peru. It was one of the best decisions ever and seemed like perfect timing for this trip and where I was in my life.

Many children have a hard time in public school but are told to "suck it up." I adore people who take their children's happiness and peace into consideration.

Page 9:

Transcript -
8.22.15
I dozed off lightly. I dreamed you were walking toward me. You had a look on your face that read you thought I looked tired and in rough shape. Good to see your handsome face. I am going to see if I can find you again.

It is freezing here! I am sure I will be buying some Alpaca stuff. I am sitting next to a sign that has something inside that is making a ticking clock sound. Pa, it's 4:00 in the morning - who needs ticking at this quiet hour?

8.22.15
Pa, just landed in Cusco. Holy Moly The snow capped mountains as one flies over are Glorious. WOW! I scrambled to get my camera out. I took a couple of shots but

the settings were wrong + I got no shot. I put the dial to Auto and snapped a few.
Good morning!

8.22.15
Papa! How you say? So I am running on very little sleep at this

Notes -
I didn't research what the climate—or much of anything—was like in Peru; I imagined
it was hot all the time. I was wrong.

"How you say?" is another example of me making fun of Pa, who was making fun
of me, I used to say it a lot when I didn't know a word or was searching for a word
to use. Pa would say, "You know how to speak English. You know *how to say.*" I was
being silly, using the phrase to create emphasis and drama around what I was
sharing with him.

Page 10:

Transcript -
8.22.15
point + feel "weird". I was worried I wouldn't be able to get to Machu Picchu today.
This one tour group co at the airport said no way, it's to late. So I shopped around
and another place said it was possible, so booked with them. It cost more money
but worth it, plus they arranged all. I am staying in a hostel tonight. I can't wait to
eat meat again. This train ride is off the hook though. It has super wide windows +
glass panels on the roof. We are riding at the base of the mountains and alongside
the river. Supposedly the speckled bear can be see along the banks, not by me
though. There is soft Peruvian music playing in-the background. It is a flut "ish"
instruments. wind holes It almost sounds Asian. I met a woman from Thailand
and a dude from

Notes -
Anytime I mention "weird" in this journal, it's another occasion I am making fun
of Pa, making fun of me. Pa invited me to explore the gifts of Salvia Divinorum
tincture in June 2015, after he tried it. He wanted to compare our experiences. He

asked me how it was, so when I felt back to normal after ingesting a small amount of the tincture, I said, "I felt weird." Weird wasn't quite the data point that he, the scientist, was searching. I was too out of it to go into detail at the moment, so weird was all I could offer.

The announcer mentioned something about seeing the speckled bear, and I wrote "not by me though" because one of my greatest fears is of bears. Also, Pa made fun of the way I said "bear" because of my Boston accent. You can't tell if I am saying "bare," "beer," or "bear." Once upon a time, he bought me bear spray. I thought it was one of the nicest things anyone has ever done for me.

Page 11:

Transcript -
8.22.15
Guatemala on the train ride. Someone just said "Proborcito" (sp?).

Pa, this place is beautiful. I got some cash, going to have lunch and then take a bus to Machu Picchu. That headache is still persisting. Should I not complain about it? It's there, what is saying it is there going to do? I do wonder if it's because I haven't had any meat. It is so cold in Cusco! I am in "Watertown" right now. The natives are so cute. They look like photos I have seen. It's weird that they wear the same thing - I mean all of them that dress this way. It is standard issue gear!

Notes -
Pa and his sister, who have a beautiful relationship, have an inside joke about "*pobrecito*," which in Spanish means "poor little thing." I think it's meant to be sarcastic. He used to say it to me when we first started dating. "(sp?)" is my way of saying I question the spelling on this.

When I first arrived in Peru, I saw many older women dressed this way. As time went on, I found, there were many women of all ages who wear this type of clothing. There are photographs in the journal that show the clothing better than my terrible drawing. See page 36 for a photo.

<u>Transcript</u> -

8.22.15

I am pooped today! I can't wait to be able to eat meat again. The woman, Carol, who booked my tour said not to eat meat after I told her why I came to Peru.

The dude from Guatemala tried hiking the mountains around here. He said he couldn't breathe and turned around. He showed us the trail - sucker was high up. He said he walked for 2 hours upstairs, then decided he had enough + then he walked downstairs for 2 hours. He tried.

I hope you are writing your movie. This is weird not being able to talk to you least 10 times before noon. I miss you but I know I have all this new stuff to distract me. You are home. It is like that when you go to NY but that is only for a weekend.

Notes -

After this trip to Peru I made chili, but soon after realized that I didn't want to eat meat anymore. Pa let me know afterwards that he read that many "psychonauts" report the same experience.

As part of preparing for the cleanse and to sit with Mama Ayahuasca, it is suggested that you not eat meat and not drink alcohol or caffeine; you should wear light-colored clothing, set intentions, and practice meditation, among other things.

<u>Transcript</u> -

8.22.15

This is the view from the cafe I had lunch at, today. Some of the huge rocks in the water are so smooth. I think you would like it here. I not only miss you for the obvious reasons but you have a beautiful mind and you see things in a different way than I do or most others do. I like hearing your thoughts on things.

I haven't felt any special feelings since flying in over the snow capped mountains. Pa, I am nervous that you are going to find this boring, much like those who find boring looking at photos of other's boring ass vacations.

This is the toughest time - dinner time. The longest I am away from you is for work, but by day's end, I am with you again. So this sucks.

Notes -
There were some posts online that told about "special energy" found in Peru, especially at the ruins. I was in search of the energy I read about, so I suppose I had expectations and was being mindful of experiencing anything out of the ordinary. When I mentioned "special feelings" here, it is actually referring to that energy.

Page 14:

Transcript -
8.22.15
So I just came down from Machu Picchu (correct sp!). It was a sight to behold pa! The shots I took for you didn't come out very well. The animals did. The selfie sticks were plentiful today. The place is way up. We kept climbing and climbing. I was disheveled. Some guides are available which I think would make it more interesting. I didn't get a guide. I had a really tough time with the heights. I almost left! Talk about wanting you with me. There are dogs everywhere! Perros. I am eating sopa ... mushroom sopa.

This guy I asked for soda water went to the store and got some. I saw him run out for it and run back with it. I was pumped - had limes and all!

Notes -
It was tough to be way up there among so many people. The place was packed, and it is overwhelming to move about busloads of people, in just as much a confused state as me as to where to go. I really did think about hopping right back on a return bus. I breathed, collected myself, and pushed on. If I can do it, anyone can.

On the morning I departed, I left Pa a bunch of sticky notes around the apartment. One of them read "Is there *even* any soda water where I am going?" I was drinking it a lot, at the time. Now, I drink a lot of Kombucha too. I like fizzy drinks.

Page 15:

8.22.15
wait for it: it has some kind of additive I didn't know. Soda water w. x. I looked at the ingredients and it had corn syrup in it; I stopped reading after that. I did tip him but felt bad still. I poured most out in the bushes so he would think I drank it. I had to. LOL!

photo covered dinner jizz
my dinner

It's weird to see when going by a construction sight to see dudes with shovels and wheel barrels. I just witnessed a couple break up. She gave him all his shit from her duffle bag and a key. There was no yelling, just fast irritated movements. Some dude is moving - using a 2 wheeler. Pa, we've got it made. I guess I should only speak for me. I got it made. I have all I need and more. nI have you and we have the minds we do. Aw, dumped dude just went into the restaurant I am at to get plastic bags for all his shit.

Notes -
When I read, if I spill food on the page I am reading, I write what caused the stain, near the stain on the page. I like to buy used books and think that if the books I own get sold or passed on, I'd like the reader to know what the stains are. I used the word *jizz* because Pa would use that word, if he spilled something.

I explained to Pa that moving with the two-wheeler was pretty intense. It wasn't just a box of clothing from a car to the doorstep; these men were moving beds and large items down the road, and I could not see their destination. Some of this moving was done uphill too. It was incredible to see it done with such ease and normalcy.

When I wrote about the construction site, I didn't make it clear that there seemed to be no power tools or machinery. These sites were places where significant work was being done, and the workers used basic tools.

8.22.15
I don't feel well at all - stupid headache! You know I can be a baby and I want to be home now and have you take care of me. I ate fish for dinner. I wanted to feel full ... finally.

Chinese people be touring pa. I am afraid something is wrong. the headaches.

such pressure

I was being mindful to see if I noticed any special energy at MP. I thought I did at first but then nothing. I don't really dig being around all those people. It was pretty crowded.

That dude on the train told me that they (the Peruvians) grow over 1000 different types of potatoes. I need to look that shit up. It doesn't seem possible.

Did I mention I want to come home?

Notes -
I made note of Chinese people because of all the people I see touring, they look most professional. These are the folks in all (or any combo) of the following: dressed in layers, wearing a smart head covering and sometimes an umbrella, toting a good-looking camera, carrying backpacks/fanny packs, as well as being well equipped with a selfie stick. The way I wrote it in the journal is my ghetto version of relaying this thought.

Page 17:

8.22.15
The chick from the break up just walked by the scene of the break up.

I don't feel that special-ness I felt when home with you thinking of how it would be. I am going to try an attitude adjustment. This is at the trip of a lifetime. I can do better than this. I am going to try to be upbeat even though my head feels like it will explode!

Getting or waiting to get a head, neck, + shoulder massage. Hopefully it helps. [I miss you] It helped in the moment but then it didn't. I walked around a bit. There are cool hidden streets or back streets like QC. It was nice to walk along until the shops repeat and so do brokers on behalf of the shops trying to get you in there.

I thought this would be cool but I want to talk to you. I want you to talk to me. I want to hear your voice. Not that weird whisper thing you do in my ear but your regular talking voice.

Notes -
I really felt awful with this persisting headache.

Page 18:

Transcript -
8.22.15
I am two hours plus away from my hostel. I have to take a train, bus, and then a cab. I hope I can knock out on the train. It will be interesting to see all in the dark now. I hope I get a window seat.

I am enjoying a spot of mint tea. I will have to pee soon. Aren't you glad of these updates? dead bug

Pa, I have been very mindful lately. I have tried to come up with ways to show my love for you. Some how don't want to write "just" it's not saying I love you isn't (or doesn't seem like) enough. That is part of why the passion has come into play as of late.

LOL everywhere I look behind me, there is a big ass mountain behind me. This place is like the dessert. It gets pretty fuckin cold at night.

Tomorrow is the big day. At 2pm

Pa and I attended a yearly outdoor festival called Jerry Jam, which we were on our way to making a tradition. It was so much fun watching Grateful Dead cover bands, although there were a few groups that fell flat. I started noticing such things after not drinking alcohol for a while. There was one band that stood out as lacking passion and seemed to just be going through the motions. After seeing that, it occurred to me that I wanted to be mindful of being passionate.

Page 19:

Transcript -
8.22.2015
I get picked up from the airport to go to the retreat center. I think it will be a lot better. I will be away from the maddening crowds ... lol.

I haven't slept in a bed since Thurs. Pa, want to relearn Spanish with me and solely speak that at home for a spell? That would be a major challenge and productive.

I was so done in this town hours ago but I have an assigned train + seat and the bus + cab are lined up timed with this schedule. Fingers crossed all is lined up. It's a 2 hr train ride and at least 1/2 hour bus. Not sure about the cab.

2:00 am 8/23/15
Pa, I am in the Hostel. I am having a panic attack. I don't know why. I wish I could say I am being brave but I just cried like how you say? A bitch. I am breathing though, calming down. I am

Notes -
I wonder if others get down in the dumps while traveling alone. I was extremely exhausted. Afterwards, I had a renewed sense of life with Pa, with the passion, as well as recently having surgery. I began looking at life very differently. I voluntarily left to make even more improvements for me and for us. I had a strong feeling that it was important for our future.

Transcript -

8.23.15

going to hop in bed with Tappan and think of you. I love you. Good night. I miss you. I feel better. I wish you could hold me. Someone writing a review in one place I was looking into said nice but you can hear the dogs all through the night barking. I can. I think everyone can - there are dogs everywhere. I wish I could take one home. I feel better. Buenos noches, mi amor! 44, sleeping with a stuffed monkey ... hay dios mio.

Good morning, Buenos dias I have no idea what time it is. It feels like about 6am. The dogs were awake for sure earlier than now. It's Sunday - this place has holy people - that scares me right now. I have a feeling of that being a dangerous thing. I think I had a dream about collectivism and someone telling me how we are all one but how individualism is key. Key to what I can't put

Notes -

"Tappan" is a sock monkey I bought for Pa one Valentine's Day. I started bringing it with me, to keep me company while I travelled, especially on road trips. I have a fear of driving over bridges, so I would put the monkey on my lap while going over them. I used to wipe the sweat of my palms on the monkey, and it afforded me a bit of comfort. Pa witnessed this one time and named the monkey "Tappan," after we drove over the Tappan Zee Bridge in New York.

I sound ignorant writing about holy people in this way. Again, generalizing is not something I am fond or proud of. I am not a fan of organized religion, and hearing these folks triggered a disdain of religion.

Transcript -

8.23.15

into words but it was as deep as existing. I was listening to two friends talk and they were feeding off of one another. Man they had a lot of judgement. I was thinking in my head (usually where thinking happens) that one day they would found out that they don't need each other to validate the others existence. That is what it seemed like. They

(3 young men) agreed with one another and piled the judgements on. They seem to flow as one and there is security in that. One day, they may break from that. I have to think more on this like how I may use collectivism as security - being with you, anarchism, the FSP. The FSP is a great example: I felt the security until I see the holy people, Keeniacs, and maybe Poly peeps. Their individual group threatens that security. I will swap out poly peeps for minarchists. It is like when you said you would work

Notes -
Ironically, wasn't I judging them? I realize that I was making the observation to understand some things, but judgment was present. Some say we judge every day to be able to interact with others in a safe way,. I think of it now, and having looked up the definition, judging seems just fine. I guess it depends on how it's done. These men were gossiping and being unkind.

I still think about this. I believe that we are all *one,* but we each bring something unique to the *oneness.* We are still individuals. Being connected doesn't take away from who were are. I believe I was thinking about it like the Borg of *Star Trek: The Next Generation.* If I had to guess, I think the oneness is to assure we all live happy and peacefully without interfering with the happiness and peace of others. For now, for me, my contribution is to help people. Again, I suggest looking within. I suggest self-exploration to find *your* answers.

I went to Peru as an atheist. After my experience, I believe there is something that could be called a god. I don't use that term. I use *source* or *the one.* I think of *the one* as energy. I think of it like the *force* from *Star Wars.* My apologies if you don't get these sci-fi references. *Star Wars* seems most like what is real to me.

Page 22:

Transcript -
8.23.15

with the socialists to end was or whatever you agreed with them about until they started trying to sell you/force on you socialism. Maybe it holds true for being with you too. I feel secure until we disagree, it is better or would be for me to see reality, we are not one unit. We are individuals who will disagree at some point. (Many even)

Back to these scary holy people. They are ringing bells for long periods of time. It stopped only to be replaced by singing (holy singing). oh yea, and the rooster - arghhhh!

Notes -
I am not totally against socialism; just don't force me to participate through the government. If a group wants to voluntarily participate, I am all for it, for them.

I am not proud writing about being afraid of the holy people. My apologies. I guess it's true that people may fear what they don't understand. I now have more tolerance for this sort of thing because of what I believe, which isn't very concrete. I am still gathering information and learning new things all the time. I like what one said, that perhaps it's best to have fluid thinking.

The worst typo in this has to be me writing "worst" for "worse." Ernie Hancock has historically been the early morning broadcast personality at a camping trip we attended yearly named Porcfest. Each morning, Ernie would screech a morning greeting into the microphone that broadcast through a loudspeaker. It doesn't make him a bad guy, just annoying. His show is *Freedom Phoenix.*

Pa said he wanted to get a waterbed. He also said he wanted satin sheets to go with it. I never could tell if he was serious or not. He settled for a Tempurpedic I bought for us, extra firm, per his request.

Page 23:

Transcript -
8.23.15
There is no god - if so, I would have water in my room. What to do? I found a mujer to help me - the water was off.

I heard "Love me do" on the way from the train station to the bus stop. I just woke up from a lil nap. It was so late - early - and we were all jammed in the wee bus. I laughed out loud + it caused me to make myself feel joy. like so. There were brits on the bus + I swore I heard one (both crossed out) say outloud "The Beatles". Going to wear my love shirt today.

I just heard the tune that plays at the start of one of Immortal's songs. I was like, yeah, I am in Peru.

Good news, no headache! <u>Grateful</u>!! I met an old dude who gave me his card. He was super earthy and knew no English. He gave me his card. I thought he was selling me an Ayahuasca type experience, I don't know. I will show you his card. I (heart) you. I love you when I feel bad. (panic attack). I love you when I feel good. (now)

<u>Notes</u> -
This seems disrespectful, although in jest. My apologies.

"My love shirt" refers to a tank top I bought for the trip. I was inspired after watching the Beatles documentary, before the trip. It has the lyrics of the song "All You Need Is Love" printed on it. I believe this is true and think I really get the meaning after meeting Mama Aya and all of my experiences during the shamanic cleanse.

This elderly dude was a traditional-looking Peruvian. His card had a picture of earth, air, water, and fire on it. He kissed me on the cheek, but I didn't feel creeped out. I felt like it was a blessing, and I was grateful. I believe we communicated enough for him to realize I was there to meet Mama Ayahuasca. I felt the blessing was for that reason.

Page 24:

<u>Transcript</u> -
8.23.15
I [This is like how I say a sentence that sounds like one word.] went to a farmer's market. It is like that big ass one in Phillie. There are vendors inside and all around on the streets. This one was selling fresh cut pineapple. You know I bought some. Yum. Some dude and I laughed at me because I almost dropped a big piece at one point. I caught it and laughed. The lady next to this lady (a pic) said 5 soles for the photo. I gave her $1 and they laughed. Good story for them, maybe? I snapped a photo of her and gave it to her. It is interesting that in a place that is supposed to be a 3rd world country or whatever (U.S. is more developed) they have all this fresh produce + meat so readily available.

Notes -
The market in Philly is named the Reading Terminal Market, and the one in Cusco, Peru, is the San Pedro Market. The one in Peru is filled with fresh fruits, nuts, meats, and all sorts of other foods and handmade goods. A highlight of our adventure was to visit the market one day, and one of the facilitators pointed us to the fruit smoothie stands. There is such a wide, delicious variety. In the Philly market, I found the joy of scrapple (back when I ate meat).

Page 25:

Transcript -
8.23.15
Do they have a meat regulator like the USDA? It doesn't seem so. They sell shit right in the open. Stick ya hand sanitizer up your bum! (Sterile U.S.A.) nosa but kind of I found someone selling nuts. I got a little snack pack of almonds, pecans, + yellow raisins. [I wonder if raisins got their name from "Rays of the Son (sun) ? Ray-ins Tee hee] It costs 15 soles. That is pricey, considering I spent 30 or 35 soles on a sweater. I shared a handful of the mix with a scruffy looking dude at the airport. He took it. I wonder what it would be like to share with an American that way?

Bloody headache came back. I drank some chamomile tea and that seemed to help for a spell but then it didn't. Cocsucker is back.

Notes -
I could probably share my food with another person in the United States. Would I try, though? I am not sure; perhaps. It was simple and natural when I did it in Peru.

I like my theory, but it's way off and sounds like the ramblings of someone who experienced the gifts of cannabis, which isn't a bad thing.

Page 26:

Transcript -
Some other photos I took at the CCHU They didn't come out that good.

These are some photos taken at the sacred ruins. My nickname for Machu Picchu was "the Cchu."

Page 27:

8.23.15
Pa, good news, I am going to live! I have altitude sickness Maybe the headache at home was a premonition. Siracha LOL, that isn't the name but it is something close to it is the Spanish name for it actually. I am (happy crossed out) relieved that I know what is going on.

Good night, Pa! I love you.

Good morning, pa. I went to bed at 8:00pm, so up at the crack ass. The stars were shining bright and now they are not in sight. The sky is different hues of blue with a bit of white.

The woman who owns the meditation center was born in Belgium, grew up in Greece (Greek Islands) and then moved to Peru. Her meditation teacher asked

Notes -
I was close! Altitude sickness is known as "*soroche*" in Peru. This is a good example of some of the misinformation in this journal. It may be best to verify anything you question. Another example is the number of potato varieties; some said two thousand different kinds of potatoes, but I have seen online that there are up to five thousand different types. It makes me think of looking within for truth. It's what this Ayahuasca ceremony was, essentially. It was like my own verification.

By this point, I and a small group of guests had been picked up at the airport by the facilitators and driven to the retreat center in vans. Some guests were already there, having arrived in cabs. As I revise this, I realize how wonderful it was of Coby and CJ to join the drivers in picking us up at the airport. There was only one person left, who arrived a few days later. Everyone was super friendly, and the group had a *mom*, who explained how we would get our drinking water. I was grateful for that.

Transcript -

8/24/15

her to run some meditation retreats in Peru and that was what brought her here. She built this center and here she is. She sold two houses in Greece before she moved - before the turmoil, for sure! Her parents owned a hotel on the Islands, which helped her learn the business. This place is glorious, pa. She had a fence built all the way around the house/grounds/meditation hall. That is the bomb because the surrounding homes, etc. are not as nice, so with the fence, beauty is encapsulated. It is flipping freezing.

Today, the 13 of us will be split into two groups. One will go into town to shop + the other will stay and work with tobacco. When I do, I will take a shot of tobacco that is so concentrated, if left in my stomach would kill me. [god damn 7 litres] So, I will have to drink water to induce vomiting. It is meant to clear the throat of all blockages.

So, [I do that a lot] I had a most delicious [it was!]

Notes -

I wrote that the tobacco ceremony is to clear the throat, but others say it helps purify the liver and the respiratory system, as well as clarify thoughts and emotions. I never imagined I would publish this book, so these details were less important to me, as I was living in the moment.

Transcript -

8/24/15

yoga practice this morning. This guy [Coby] said we were having a yoga high or got a yoga high. I walked mindfully to a spot where there was a great view of the mountains and continue mindfully. So I did. I sat for a bit. I meditated for a bit. I decided to lay down for a bit. I was lying there "coaching myself" to just notice. I noticed a buzzing sound. I continued to coach myself telling myself to simply notice. I thought the buzzing was bees and then through better ... flies. Then another "just notice" ... then "is that shit I smell?" It was shit. LOL I moved.

Hey, Pa! I am having a hell of a time here. I did my tobacco cleanse - tons of water [7 liters of H2O] and throwing up. Good thing I had all that practice with appendicitis. If it wasn't for the surgery, I would not be here right now. I also had my coca leaf reading. It was

Notes -
Coby was right on!

When I told the stern owner of the place this story, she burst into laughter. That was cool, as she seemed quite serious.

At the tobacco cleanse, I was introduced to the medicine music known as *Icaros*. The shaman let us know that some offer Mama Aya without going through this type of cleansing, and that can be dangerous. Preparation is very important. They instructed us to ask Pachamama, which is what Peruvians lovingly call Mother Earth, to accept our vomit and the toxins that came with it from us as we poured it into the ground. I used to look at Earth as a place I lived, not as something I was connected to and provided for me. I was (and still am) grateful. Before this trip, I had an emergency appendectomy and threw up most of the night before, so I was well practiced in vomiting.

Page 30:

Transcript -
8/24/15
quite fascinating! [And a massage. It was by this dude Jose who is Doris's man. He is like 20 years, at least, younger. Most of the women were "gaga" over him. LOL He is a hottie] By the leaves, I am on the right path. Holy cow she picked out a leaf that was John and said you are glad you got rid of that one. He was not right for you. She showed me you and me. She said you are beautiful, we are alike, and you are proud, love, and adore me. I need to work on the insecurity and the stories in my mind. The good news is that I am. [She said to look into creating art. not so much painting or traditional but look for beauty. She said I am a great spirit.] She said I have great abundance and I don't need to worry about the future or money. She said that I am on earth to help people. She said I am on the right path and that I will help many people and make $ too. She said I shouldn't brag about how great you are because people become envious. She said we are very much alike.

Pa I feel as though this was the right thing for me to do. I

John was not right for me, nor I for him. I must have been a really difficult challenge for him, and for that, I apologize. I am grateful for all I learned and hope he left the relationship with some lessons.

If you bought this book, you helped make this come true by doing so. Thank you for buying this book and being open enough to give it a read.

Page 31:

<u>Transcript</u> -
8/24/15
believe we will be even better and more connected than ever. Thank you for your incredible love and support. I have said these things but I want you to really know. She said that I should take you to one of these things. Shaman Cleanse I said I wanted to do all to get you to one. She said no, go do it together. So, I will ask you what you would like to do.

Pa, this is getting real!

I didn't tell you about the coca ceremony from last night. We chanted a bit. We picked out leaves that were "perfect" for us. We ran them along our hands asking the leaves to take what we want to shed. Then, we brought them outside + gave them to the earth [mother earth]. We chose a few more after that and set intentions again for what we wanted to get rid of and burned them in the fire. We sat

<u>Notes</u> -
This could not have been more true. Pa and I worked on our relationship and improved by giving up things, especially alcohol. The shamanic cleanse changed me, and he could not deny the changes. He was also affected by them. It was another new start for us. There was more peace between us because I was more at peace. It's true what is said that if you want to change the world, change yourself.

Everything was done in ceremonial fashion and with intention. There was also an honoring of Mother Earth. I was happy to learn this because it felt right and good to honor the Earth and her offerings in this way. It felt natural.

Page 32:

<u>Transcript</u> -
8/24/15
in a circle, went around the room and said who we were and what we were doing here. I said something like to get out of the shadow of my past, what society thinks I should be, and what my parents want for me. Also to shed what didn't serve me so I can reach my full potential. OR something like that.

I had lunch. They use beans + rice as filler so I don't get to eat much. Pa, I don't feel bad being away from you or doing my best to stay present. This will be great for you and for me. I am happy I am having this wild experience.

Pa, I am super tired though. I think I am going to bed now. I love you. Good night. I love you so much. I miss you like crazy. 3 days down. I am so glad I have this book and can tell or talk to you

<u>*Notes*</u> -
Even after I told everyone why I was there, I didn't feel satisfied with my answer. I thought it was made up, like something I read or heard and regurgitated. I reread my journal and think that it made sense, but I truly didn't know the reason I was there. I didn't feel comfortable saying that I was simply drawn there, which was the truth.

When I took the trip to Peru, I was eating mostly according to the Paleo diet. At present, I am not eating meat and don't eat corn or rice, but I do eat beans. I was wafting back and forth with eating meat and dairy, but then I watched the movie *Cowspiracy* and realized Pachamama needs help; we must honor her and treat her well. She needs us, and we need her. Neither is to be used; we are connected.

All the learning and revelations can really take it out of one. My mind was changing in real time and being blown away, as outer layers were crumbling to the ground.

8/24/15
even though I can't talk to you in person. I think that is huge. I recall being away from you before and that was a big deal - "I wish I could tell pa this" or that. We pulled leaves off of plants today and put them in a big pot to boil. Then I brought a bucket in the shower and poured it over my head. Those were supposed to be done outside but it's freezing out, now. Fuck that, buddy. I got a massage today too. So, it was yoga, meditation, tobacco ceremony, leaf reading, and massage. oh, + plant bath. <u>Hell of a first day.</u>

8/25/15
Good morning, pa.

I slept well for the first half of the night but not the last. The dreams, pa. Holy cow!! I had a bad thought that maybe you wouldn't miss me at all. Then, I had this dream that I was stuck in the

Notes -
I didn't exactly get the concept of the plant baths, at first. I poured the bath over me when it would have been better to rub it over my body, like soap.

It was, indeed, one hell of a first day. I was changed at this point and exhausted by all the changes. There was only a little time to process it all before new ideas and concepts were introduced as well as tasks associated with the cleanse ceremony.

8/25/15
hospital for a spell. I got out and made it to you but you didn't seem to care too much that I was there. This is the part of dreaming that I don't really miss. The ones where I get affected emotionally. You know? I am way, I have the fear a little bit and then I have that dream. It is not good, pa. Pa, I think speaking/learning to speak Spanish in the home could be a really good thing. Also, perhaps we can learn other languages in the same way. That sounds awesome to me.

Today will be a along day. We are going on an all day excursion - shopping and then a trip to some ruins. I guess these ones are not as touristy as the other ones. That is good because the crowds of people are too much sometimes. Who am I kidding, all the time.

Notes -
Prior to traveling to Peru, I enjoyed the benefits of cannabis on a daily basis. It helped me sleep. It worked really well, but I found that I didn't dream much. When I was in Peru, not receiving its gifts, I dreamed a lot, and they seemed to be wild and so real. It was unsettling to have dreams where emotions run high, especially so far from my love. I see now, there was no need to take it personally or let those feelings get to me.

Page 35:

Transcript -
8/25/15
I am getting your crystal necklace. He is searching for the right one for you. (As I wrote)

Pidita - spiritual
Aquamarine - relaxation
black tourmaline - protection & healing
Chicana Serpentine - power

Hey papa! I haven't talked to you all day. I joked at dinner how I don't even need a bf, I can just write to a made up one. LOL. Nah, I may not need you but I want you. I choose you. I hope you are at peace, papa. I did some incredible hiking feet today. It was so high up, a woman I am in the retreat with who did it yesterday was concerned that I would have a hard time coming down. People + we took cabs up the mountain and hiked down.

Notes -
We went to shop in the town of Pisaq, where we were directed to a crystal shop where a man named Uturunku sells crystals. These are the crystals in the necklace he picked for Pa. More on that later.

It was funny to have felt comfort in talking to Pa when it was in a journal. I was thankful for the process because I was missing him terribly.

I was very afraid of heights. This was helpful in becoming less so. I went skydiving to try to help, but it didn't. On the cab ride up, I found some relief from using a technique called "ETF tapping."

Page 36:

<u>Transcript</u> -
8/25/15
So, [I want to stop this] this is the first thing I saw when we came to the start of the ruins. They are so cute and I didn't realize that this is the norm. I thought there would be a few but no, they are all over the place. This is a photos of the ruins. They are wild. Opposite the ruins are these mountainous spots with rocks piled and then there are holes in them. They are freaking graves. The holes show that the graves were robbed.

I love you. You would have been proud of me.

<u>*Notes*</u> -
The photos show images of men and women in traditional dress. I drew something similar on page 11.

Page 37:

<u>Transcript</u> -
8/25/15
Pa, these people talk about going back into the matrix. Much ... WOW!

I thought about taking a cab back down the mountain. I didn't. So, we got in cabs early in the morning and went off to Pisaq. There were seven of us. This wonderful woman, I told you about going to her retreat center in Troncones, CJ (Ananda), told us where to shop and how to barter and all that. She told us about the crystal shop. We were to meet her at this mexican restaurant at 1pm. So we shopped and shopped - I found all I wanted but bought my sweater too small + I didn't like the color I picked for you. [I wore it one night + like it.] They looked good up on hangers.

I went to the crystal shop and picked out 2 laboradorite pieces for me. Then I asked him to choose one for me (he does this) and it meant something to me. I asked him to pick one out for you too. He did and I hope it means something to you. I adore the pants I got for you. I hope you dig them.

Notes -
Pa and I did a lot of volunteer work in the liberty movement and talked about being out of the Matrix. This would be someone who knew the political system and society are designed to enslave us. On the trip, some folks in my group were talking about *The Matrix*. It was then I realized that my world view was getting ready to be shattered, once again. It seemed like another level of the *rabbit hole*.

Shopping was fantastic. It wasn't so crowded as many places can be, and the ruins were a nice treat. I felt like we had VIP treatment and knew of the road less traveled. With CJ as our guide, we were directed to the best places. And I don't mean cream of the crop in a material sense but in good vibes, top-notch places.

I think Uturunku did an incredible job picking out crystals that mean something to me and for Pa. Pa seemed like he was less spiritual, having a scientist mind, so the spiritual crystal seemed very appropriate for him. It wasn't until later that I realized I was wrong; he was very spiritual, just not the kind of spiritual I was. He was big-time spiritual through nature and music. I am glad I was able to see that, eventually.

Page 38:

Transcript -
8/25/15
We met for lunch - soup, stir fry, Peruvian Mint tea, and plantains for dessert. What a perfect meal it was. Pa, I puked and they puked several times in front of each other - so we bonded. Then, it was off to the ruins. We rode up and got right to it. Pa, these ruins keep climbing + climbing. It was nuts. I was "coaching" myself. I said at one point: "Luke had to face his father Darth Vader, I can do this. And I DID. It was cool. There was a high energy - I felt the walls vibrating - subtly. This woman called us over to the "room" she could feel energy. We all went in lied down and did some breathing

I felt like the sharing of our tobacco ceremony bonded us. It was interesting to share something so intense with a group of people who just met; we were in such a vulnerable state. We surrendered to the process and made it through, together.

Talking about Luke and Darth Vader was another *Star Wars* reference. Pa thought it was clever of me to think of it in this way.

Page 39:

Transcript -

8/25/15

and connected with the earth. We were laying there on our backs and it was raining on us. What an incredible experience with all. There was more bonding. It was super cool. No one is ever like, well this is weird. It is so cool and open. I am pooped after all this - we climbed down the mountain on trails. My knee (left) was dogged. Doris, the leaf reader said my knees are/will be trouble for me. It took awhile and there was a lone flute - like instrument playing for us and travelled down the mountain playing for us. [One song was a Simon & Garfunkel.] That thing We got to the bottom and went "home". I had and awesome dinner and chat. The other half of the group did their tobacco ritual, so we caught up. Then it was time for song time. Take a guess as to what that is … I am eating it, now. BITTER!!!

Notes -

This was such a special moment for me. I really did connect with the Earth after the ritual of giving her what I purged or asking her to take it from me. I was held by her, it felt.

I don't like that I wrote "Doris, the leaf reader." I did think it would help Pa know who I was talking about, but it would have been more to my liking if I gave her the respect she deserves in this writing. I know it's not that deep, and she probably wouldn't mind, but she means a lot to me, and I would like to have demonstrated that.

In case you didn't guess, I was eating chocolate.

Transcript -

8/25/15

I miss you, papa. I am going to bed now, pa. I love you. I might read a bit 1st

8/26/15

Good morning, pa. Damn, I am up and at 'em because a radio withe a talking dude is blaring outside. It is staticky too so super annoying. WTF? What to do? I am going to read a bit. Either someone made a terrible mistake or is not so considerate.

It stopped but I am up! This was a different kind of species of cock - cocksucker!

Pa, I made the shop keeps @ the chocolate store laugh. I took a sample of chocolate outside of the store to taste. Someone was holding a tray of samples. I wanted dark and she followed me in to help. She did by getting the chocolate and quoting me a price. Another person took a tray and was headed out. He corrected her and the price was more than she said. I said ok but I am going

Notes -

This was awful. The person was playing music and a pre-recorded message, over and over again. Someone said it was the trash collector.

Page 41:

Transcript -

8/26/15

to take more of this - and dipped into his sample tray. We all laughed.

I had a dream that you and I lived at someplace that was an extension or satellite sight of the quill. We were frustrated because we wanted more. (More what - not sure but that was the feel). You were going on about how Merav was saying that these people just don't get it. Not sure what "it" was. I have been dreaming in a way that seems to create a dilemma or situation where some decisions need to be made or there will be some outcome because of action but I don't find out what that is. It's weird. I also dreamed that I was tagged in a post on FB accused of killing someone. It was by that dude Blake Anderson (the dude who knew all or most of the lines in shit, what is that move? - I can't even remember the famous line. You. Wolf of Wall Street Whew - did it.

Notes -

Just to be sure you get the joke, I took more samples from the tray to offset the discrepancy between the price I was originally quoted and the correct price. If Pa had to listen to me explain, just to make sure he knew how funny I think I am, you do too.

Before I left for Peru, I bought three journals. One of them was to become a dream journal. I have had some really interesting ones and am glad I got into the habit of documenting them.

Page 42:

Transcript -
8/26/15
I really believe I should give up weed now. I am going to explore my dreams and foster them. [I peeled the cactus, as did my bros + sisters. Cut the greenest bits off. First some people clipped the pricks off with the nail clippers. Itrst some peo High.]

Even though the dreams are weird, I miss you less or rather feel less lonely if I am dreaming of you. I didn't like the first few but last nights' was more comforting.

Pa, this is what I feel and was telling you 8/27 (started talking to another wonderful person and stopped writing).

8.27.15
Papa, [Good morning!] Holy moly. I did the Washuma ceremony. We drink cactus "cactus ctus s. a cemony. was telling yo Then, the magic started to happen. I remember being very attached to my puke bucket and carrying it around withe me, not sure what to do. Doris said being very attached to my puke bucket and carrying it around wit I got some smoke

Notes -
"Weed": I can't believe I have called such a wonderful plant medicine this. It is disrespectful. There are many movies that make it seem like a joke. It seems abused

to me, as the Earth has been. It affords me pain relief, relaxation, and sleep, and it opens my mind. Surely, I can call it cannabis. Along with passion came the inquisition about how I was viewing and treating the things around me. I want to mean it. I want to mean life. I want to celebrate cannabis. I recall Pa helping me see the light. He essentially asked me about giving honor to all these other medicine plants and not so much to cannabis. Thank you, Pa.

It would have been better for me to give Huachuma more respect than calling it a "cactus smoothie." I sure honored it in the moment, writing it a letter. The letter was written in my journal, so forgive the errors: "Dear Washuma, Thank you for giving me sight. I see that everything is perfect. I want water & chocolate. I am so happy I got to talk to Bonita. I got to tell her how perfect everything is. I kind of want to say how foolish I have felt but I don't feel that either. Every twig, every branch is perfect. It's all in harmony—the wind, all of it. Me, you, all of it. Time is perfect—the timing is perfect. every rock. Just notice—I have no complaints—no list—no limits. Why didn't I know this? Thank you dear Washuma for teaching me this. Colors, it's all about the colors. The colors of the mind, heart, and soul. It is about seeing the imperfections as they perfectly are. Let go of *supposed*."

It is said that the plant is a great teacher, and I feel I learned a lot. I am grateful.

Page 43:

Transcript -
8.27.15
Rape` (calms the mind, ground, and clears the path in the nose) thing blown up my nose. Hold on, after I puked, I sat for a bit and looked around. Everything seemed brighter, I could see all the ants and flying bugs more clearly. It was unbelievable. I felt "weird". I kept laughing and laughing because I kept thinking of you and "weird". Anyway, I didn't really know what to do with myself, so I hopped in the hammock. I spent most of the day in the hammock. It was glorious! Pa, I was seriously "tripping balls". Washuma is out of the world. I was laying there and so much made sense. I realized everything is perfect. It was a big revelation. It is also what Doris (said like Dorice) was telling me. There is nothing wrong. Everything is right. It is. It is the mind my mind that fills up with views of non-perfection. I also

Rapé is a tobacco snuff that is said to restore balance, ground, and calm, and it helps overcome addictions. I didn't notice its effects in Peru, as I was surrounded by mountains, practicing two hours of meditation and yoga daily, and working with other medicines. It wasn't until I got home and was back in the grind that I found how powerful this medicine is. I sat with it for one hour the first time, setting intentions, lighting Palo Santo, and listening to Icaros (medicine music). I told Pa it felt like I meditated an hour per day, for a week straight.

Remember what I explained on page 10? It holds true here. I felt "weird."

Again, I wish I gave more respect than using the words "tripping balls" to explain my experience, but that is plain language which everyone can understand. The medicine gives such lessons and resets the mind, in a way. It helped me understand that I had been creating problems where there were none. I was clouding my mind with stuff. I had the power to change everything, and all I had to do was decide that is what I wanted. It seems easier to experience this on a weeklong journey in Peru. When I got back to the States, things would get a bit escalated or complicated, in my mind. I started saying that I would "Doris it." To me, that means take all the complicated bullshit and throw it out. Make it as simple as possible, and let that be the standard. Simplify! It started with Doris teaching me that on a human level and then the Huachuma teaching me on the soul level. I am grateful.

Page 44:

Transcript -
8/27/15
let go of what is "supposed" to be. [It showed me everything has its place and it is perfect.] It was freeing! And not going to lie, trippy. I took to this woman, Bonita and checked in with her now and again. I saw a visual of what I thought was a good representation of perfection so snapped a photo and went to show Bonita. I felt like she got all that I was trying to convey. It was comforting. I would cry + laugh like crazy. I was feeling the power of love for you big time. I wished you were with me. I wanted to feel safer? Weird. But then I started feeling perfect again. It was all just fine and I went with it. I was a little too excited. You [surrendered]

It was a great feeling to let everything go. It was partly being in that state of mind and feeling so good physically, but then I took if further and thought, *Why can't I just let it all go? Why can't this be the way I am, the way I exist? Why do I need or choose to make things so hard for myself?* I decided I could let it all go, so I did.

Page 45:

Transcript -
8/27/15
know how I am. I continued to chill in the hammock. I would collect things and bring stuff into my cacoon. I got out of the hammock and chilled in the grass. People kept telling me how great I looked. It had to be a rep. of how I as feeling. See

[This woman Dawn said "Omg, how long have we been at this?" LULZ]

We spent all day on washuma. It was a long one. We were invited to have a sound bath. We went in to the temple and laid on the mats. It was wonderful. CJ's friends came. 2 dudes and a woman. One of the dudes if from Australia or New Zealand. CJ said he has like a 600 year old soul. I was listening and then started drumming with my hand on the carpet

Notes -
I had one of the best days laughing and crying in the hammock. I was crying for joy. I felt so comfortable and safe. There was a point when I was really hungry and lay in the grass, eating with a friend and talking about just about everything. It was awesome. I felt bad that I was too loud at times. I was just so damn happy and free. I found that I was free for the first time in my life. I was excited about that.

I was content to stay in the hammock, but Bonita suggested I go into the meditation hall for the sound bath. I am grateful that she convinced me to go in because it was extraordinary and the first time I'd ever heard a didgeridoo, live. I didn't know what it was before then.

Transcript -
8/27/15
Pa, all of a sudden, my hand looked like it was full on tattooed with native patterns. [looking back, it was actually the grid that I saw when on Aya. Washuma was preparing me. It showed me a little preview.] It was wild. I wasn't scared at all and kept it going. The musicians played more. I was bawling and the love was flowing. When it was over we ate. I went to find the Australian or New Zealand dude and ask him to play the Beatles song. He sang the whole thing and tried to get the melody but couldn't. He asked if I would be here next week. He would learn it and play it then. I was like, no I won't be here. But I will! This is a long time, pa. How the fuck am I supposed to go to work after this? So we went in the living room by the fire and listened and sang songs. It was magical! You would have loved it, pa. I miss you. I fee like a different person. Tomorrow is Ayahuasca day @ 9:00 am OMG.

Notes -
I was laying on my belly. I had my hand opened, facing down and moving it to the music, up and down. It was then that I saw the patterns on the back of my hand. It looked like an Alex Grey painting. The colors were absolutely beautiful and bright; they seemed almost illuminated, and my whole hand was covered.

I was crying a lot because I was so full of love for Pa, the people I was with on the trip, the people I knew back home, and all humans.

I was wrong about what day we would sit with Mama Aya. There was a trip to town in between. I actually messed up the order of this journal. Perhaps you can let go of supposed to *and* order.

Transcript -
8.27.15
We just came home from an exhausting day in the town. We went shopping, to the Cacao Museum, more shopping, and then to lunch. Holy moly am I tired and full. I

sent you and your parents a postcard. Pa, I don't want to do anymore promotion for the FSP or be in the writing club. It isn't my passion anymore.

This toilet paper was tripping me out yesterday when I was on Washuma. It was such a fun day. We are going to do it again at hot springs on Sat. That is going to be wild. What if we got a mini pinscher (sp?) ?

Notes -
It was a long day of shopping, and after exploring my mind, I could have stayed in bed all day. It was worth the trip to the cacao museum, where our hosts treated us to a heavenly fruit and chocolate fondue. It was delectable.

There were dogs all over Peru, so seeing all those adorable hounds made me long for one, even more. Our volunteering kept us really active, and we had long commutes for work, so a dog didn't make sense, but since Pa couldn't object and give me the reasons why, I kept persisting in this journal. I think I was trying to convince myself.

Page 48:

Transcript -
a workshop at the cacao museum.

Replica of a cacao tree @ the museum

Notes -
One of my favorite visits was to the chocolate museum. It had some excellent treats.

Page 49:

Transcript -
8/27/15
I am having a bad "missing you" day. There are a lot of emotions running high. I actually wanted to come home. I feel different about a few things, pa. My love for you has grown. That is for sure!!! I bought you a gorgeous poncho today. I am wearing it though. It is cold here. I think I collected a lot of good energy on/in your poncho!

I want to watch the Beatles movie again. I want our bed. I want you to hold me. I miss your voice - feet - energy - (that cool, everything is fine type energy) - I miss your face - I miss you making fun of me - I miss your take on things - I miss sharing meals with you. I miss texting you about little things here + there.

I am nervous about tomorrow but I can do it. It's why I am here.

Notes -
I am missing him terribly in this time too. My love for Pa continues to grow, interestingly enough.

Page 50:

<u>Transcript</u> -
8/27/15
Papa, I just took a plant bath outside, naked! It is almost a full moon. I was afraid to do it but then was going to have my new friend hold your poncho to voter me and do it. I decided to just do it and did. I did it quickly and it didn't seem ceremonial but rather quick. I was more focused on the naked part. I overcame a fear. That was cool. The water was warm and the plants smelled so nice.

[gift from the shop keep]

Look what I got today. This is the whistle thing I was telling you about. he he
Pa, I am going to bed. Good night, I love you.

Notes -
This was such a transformational moment. I used to have such shame for my body. I was going to do it behind cover but then I saw one of the facilitators walk out naked, to begin her ritual/ceremony. I wanted to be *that* free. Another layer of what I thought I was fell away. It was such a feeling of existing and being part of the Earth. When I got home, I didn't want to wear clothing around the house. This continued until it got really cold. Pa didn't mind this at all and was pretty impressed. I would come home from work, strip down, and start cooking. What a change.

Page 51:

8/28/15
Good morning, papa! Today is the day the Aussie guy did a great mediative practice. I am going to wear your poncho for the ceremony today. I got confirmation that "just breathing" is a good practice for this and another reason I believe the surgery was perfect. That is where I learned the mantra "all you have to do is breathe." I love you.

8/29/15
First Aya trip
Good morning, Papa. WOW! Yesterday was my new birthday. I wondered if there would be a rebirth and there was. We had the ceremony. We all gathered in a circle. We had helpers - 5 in total. We had our shaman - Salva, her mate, Adam [Adam was a finance guy. He quit it all and moved to Peru after doing Aya!], and dude from Australia x2, and a woman. First we got eyedrops to help with vision, then the powder that goes up the nose (Rape`), and then mama Aya. We were encouraged to have something warm, water, and our

[Adam liked and laughed when he saw my Freed(OM) shirt. I told him I knew why by the end.]

Notes -
My Peru trip roommate told me to breathe. It was a great reminder. She had experienced the gifts of Mama Aya before this offering. I trusted her but didn't ask too many questions. I knew that most experience Mama Aya differently. My roomie mentioned a dark side of some experiences. I focused on my intention and breathing. One can ask Mama Aya to be gentle with them, and I did. Of course I did.

I really didn't know what I was getting myself into, and I was a little nervous but more curious. It was such a calm setting. We were all in it together, even though we would journey by ourselves and were encouraged not to help our brothers and sisters because there were helpers for that. It did feel like there was supportive mental energy. We each had a space on very old, lovely tapestries.

Transcript -
8/28/15

puke bucket. I had my journal, all those things they suggested, and socks + your poncho. I wasn't scared, a little nervous but brave and mostly calm. I think I got nervous on my turn - a little shaky. It was my turn and I took 1/2 a dose. I went back to my blanket. We did this outside, surrounded by the mountains. We were to meditate for 1/2 an hour and then music started. When that happened (music) I started feeling nauseous. It seemed to take awhile but I finally puked. After that, things started getting a little out of focus and I had to lay down. Once I did, the grid appeared. I can show you pictures of what I mean. It was not a tattoo that I saw on my hand when on Washuma, it was the grid. I think it appeared to show me a preview. Pa, I was a good student. All the tools the teachers gave us, I used. I got into a fetal

Notes -
His poncho became our poncho once home, and he only wore it the one time. He looked very handsome in it, of course.

Transcript -
8/28/15

position, placing my hands on my heart and my head. I think or "was told" [by "them"] it was to help the mind ease into reality. I used it. I also used the breathe. I learned many things, like all that has been in my past has be preparation for this. I learned that it wasn't me coaching myself during my ER appendectomy, it was a spirit. He appeared when I went to the other side. He was my guide and answered any question that came up for me. I felt the presence of the teachers. I felt that many people have been helping me, whether they knew it or not. It seems on some level they knew and I felt you knew all along. I had a strong feeling that you knew - it made me laugh and cry. I laid there for hours, "learning". I realized I came here to learn. In yoga, that day, Jaya told us to surrender. I did. I learned that my PR roots are a reason I am in this space/journey faster or at this time. I learned that we were "married"

I was told by my spirit guide that the energy from the heart would travel to the mind to help it ease into what seems too much to process. It seemed to make sense and also helped.

I was told a great many things and learned much. I felt like I was "on the other side.". It was as if I were on the other side of a veil, a real existence. Many say it's simply made up in my subconscious, but for me, I think it is the most real thing ever. I think this is being kept hidden so we don't know and understand. I believe as I do and don't ask anyone else to believe me or my story. I simply ask you to consider exploring so that you find your story, truth, or what you may come to believe.

Page 54:

Transcript -
8/28/15
in the bathroom in Philly. The "energy" we felt was our union taking place. Hi, husband. You have been calling me your bride for some time. Another, you knew moment and I laughed and cried. I learned that Jaya, being very old soul, you are a couple of notches below him. "They" would like for you to come "back". They have things to teach you. I am meant to help you. They took all my fears, doubts, and things that don't serve me anymore, away. I was wondering why I seem to be calm and people around me seemed to be wailing and in pain. Rite (named him for Labradorite and a play on correct) said I don't need to do that, I have had pain enough. [I have done a lot of my work.] It is time to be free and feel good. I surrendered to it all. I felt a little alone in my space all others moved in a closer circle. I was curious about no one checking in with me but I was told that I didn't need anything. I was perfectly fine. And I was. I did get up to

Notes -
A spirit guide introduced itself to me. Upon further work at home, I learned this guide's name is Ann. Look up "spirit guide" to learn more if this is new to you. I first heard of it at a Free Your Mind conference in Philadelphia. I didn't dismiss it then but didn't research it after that. It was good to have heard of it anyway, so that I had at least heard of the concept before experiencing it.

Page 55:

Transcript -
8/28/15
jot a few things down - well one then and two when I "came back".

The one when I was "there" was the following: "No human words can prepare one for reality." ["It's not what everyone needs, it's what you need." "The journey is heaven."] The grid was intense. That place and times was intense. It seemed like flying. I breathed through it all. It's hard to say what was happening. It was an introduction to "there". It was as if I was simply being shown around. It was, how you say, orientation. I felt connected to all beings. I felt an overwhelming feeling of loving and being loved. There seemed to be many teachers along the way: You (HUGE) and small roles played by Jessica Love (by example), Mattheus (meditation + philosophy), and a bigger part by my friend, Vanessa. Others seemed to be revealed, like Bickford.

LOL, you are my husband!

It took a long time for the "reality" to sink in Rite let me know it was time to leave "there". I didn't want to go. I slowly "came to"

Notes -
The part about the teachers is interesting; looking back, they were a big impact by having tiny roles, like Jessica and Mattheus. Not knowing them very well in person, I can't think of a single word or the way they present themselves on social media that "taught" me. Vanessa is a big part of my life. She is known as the "Angelic Mom." If you search that on the web, you can get to her website. Bickford has hiked the Appalachian Trail. He had a full-time job and got free of all that to get closer to mother nature. That was a huge lesson.

Many have heard me tell the story of Pa and me first kissing in the bathroom in Philly, after an End the Fed rally. It felt like I was in the movie *The Matrix*, when they seemed to defy gravity and were floating around. There seemed to be zero gravity. When I write "They," it refers to guides on the other side or Mother Ayahuasca. I couldn't tell who was communicating to me. "They" told me that was our reunion on Earth. I asked Pa about that energy in the bathroom, and he agreed that he felt it too.

Transcript -
8/28/15
It sounds unbelievable but that is where surrendering helps. I sat up and drank a lot of water. A helper came to me and took my bottle to refill it. I thanked him like I have thanked no other. I really had a feeling of gratitude. The spirit told me to relax about using words, because they know.

For the rest of most of the day, it was about processing for me and getting used to being back in my body.

8/30/15
Pa, I miss you like crazy! (This is two days from first Aya) I love you.

Salva (the shaman) came around to do a "closing of the energy" ceremony. I told her that they gave us the perfect tools and preparation and they did. I thanked her and said "I am here to learn." She hugged me and said "Welcome to the family". It was pretty cool. I thanked the rest of the teachers and that was pretty

[It was weird because anytime I thanked somebody, they would thank me, and really mean it. Coby thanked me and my spirit. He said something about my spirit on another Washuma occasion too.]

Notes -
I had an overwhelming feeling of gratitude, and those around me all seemed to have a sense of peace. There were a few who were still struggling with the medicine. I am not sure about what they were going through or experiencing. For the most part, people were so loving and beautiful. It was like having eyes and a heart for the first time. That is what it was like for me, so that is what I thought others were feeling and experiencing; it seemed like it. I was elated.

I started eating seaweed chips; some packs are greasier than others. I was having some as a snack as I was working with the journal, and so this is seaweed snack jizz.

Doris said I have a very big spirit, and then Coby mentioned it a couple of times. I still don't really understand what that means, so that is why I made note of it. I got to thinking and wondered if it is something people just say in these circles.

Page 57:

Transcript -
8/30/15
much the day. There may be more details but I am writing this a few days later, as I wrote.

Many people swapped stories of their journey. Some were more intense than others.

2nd Washuma Trip

The next day we boarded a bus (Mercedes) headed for the hot springs for an overnight. We got to the place and the use drove us to the most beautiful spot. We did our 2nd Washuma ceremony here. I did 1/2 a cup. I chilled there and then went down the river to chill by myself. I then started to fly as a mother fucker. I was too intense for me. We started picking up and took the most

Notes -
We travelled quite a ways to Lares, Peru, to the hot springs. The scenery was spectacular and looked like the set of a movie. It looked unreal and was unlike anything I had seen in person.

I had a peaceful afternoon by a stream, but as the day went on, things got a little too intense and dark. I felt a really concentrated dark energy all around. It was a major trip to feel this when the scenery was anything but dark, and my travelmates seemed to be having a wonderful time.

Page 58:

Transcript -
8/30/15
gloriously scenic route back to our rooms. Pa, it was the most amazing scenery ever. I felt as if I as in Jurassic Park or a fairytale land. The only thing was that I was TOO

high. I was too high to eat or go down to the hot springs. I am told I as missing out on the great Full moon + stars. I was too jacked to do anything but lay in the bed. I wanted to come home so badly. I wanted you to comfort and protect me. I swore I was going home the next day, today! I still miss you like crazy and want to come home but I know I should do this. The facilitators checked on me. They were great. Coby said I don't have that much work to do and I haven't had much to do. I am wondering whether I should even do the 2ⁿᵈ Ayahuasca trip. That is tomorrow night.

Notes -
I lay in bed all night, riding out the effects of the medicine. I believe it was teaching me the whole time. It was teaching me that sometimes I will have to endure darkness by myself. Sometimes I will have to be stronger than I ever thought possible, and I can do it. People came and checked on me and gave me lime juice. I was grateful for their care and kindness. They tried to get me to come down to the springs and swim under the full moon and stars. It sounded tempting, but I believed I was to stay there with the medicine and learn what it had to teach me. I was serious about this part of my journey, and although there is no right or wrong, I wanted to do what I needed. I wanted to go in the direction I was being guided.

Page 59:

Transcript -
8/30/15
I ache to be near you. I think my bad trip was to show me that I needed to get through some things on my own. I wonder if you can sense any of what I am going through. I wonder if you made it to Hempfest. My pencil is running out, so I will leave you with "I love you".

[I went to the hot springs during the day. They were awesome. It is a mineral bath. There were different temperatures. It was so relaxing and the heat warmed my achy bones. Good times.]

8/30/15
Pa, I am so you/home sick. You are my home. You don't know how bad I just to go to the airport and take my chances trying to fly home. I was looking for an Internet cafe today, so I could send you my love in an email. This day is almost over, so it is two

more days and then I can start making my way home. I am a sad monkey without you. I just had dinner and my belly is full - finally I am full. LOL. I feel a little better but wiped out. I think I am too tired to be sad. I did pack most of my stuff -

Notes -
Wow, the hot springs were magnificent. There were many different sections, each having different temperatures. It was so relaxing and made my body feel so good. The next day, I found out that many were experiencing the medicine more intensely than they wanted to. I also found out that a fellow traveller stayed in his room the whole night as well. He was right next door. It's wild; just when you think you are alone, you are not. Someone is going through a similar situation as you.

I am very proud of myself for not leaving, like I planned to do in my head. I am grateful that I pressed on.

Page 60:

Transcript -
8/30/15
The stuff I don't need anymore. I feel like I got a ton of stuff. Pa, I was told that I should open up one of those Alpaca stores like the one in Bar Harbor, in Portsmouth. I can't wait to talk to you about it.

I am so excited to start anew again, with you. I feel like a completely different person.

Ok, I am going to read a bit and then hit the hay. 2 more days here and then travel for a day. <u>I can do this!</u> Although leaving tomorrow would be cool too. I love you!

8/31/15
Good morning, Papa! I had wild dreams, big time. I feel better about being here. I am told I will learn more if I stay + that is the reason I am here. I have some questions, like why is there a here + there. Why is there an earth and "other place". I am

Notes -
When I write "I was told," it felt as though my guide or Mama Aya was giving me information as I needed it. Answers were coming at a fast pace, and I enjoyed having all the clarity.

I was terribly excited to get home to Pa. I felt like a totally new person, with a renewed sense of love for my husband. I could feel him and his love on another level. I couldn't wait to share it all with him.

Page 61:

Transcript -
8/31/15
going back "there" tonight to learn these things and whatever else they find useful to teach me. It should be a great visit. I have a feeling that I will have to travel by myself this time and won't have a guide. I hope not but is tis what I think will happen, as of now. I am going to read, write, and drink lots of water today. I-love you! Again, thank you for all of your love and support. I am looking forward to putting my arms around you. I want you to hold me close for awhile.

Papa, I think we would be more happy if we got a dog. We can get a wee one. Remember when we both tried to draw a deer? I want ribs, SO BAD! I am going to make chili with bacon when I come home. I was going to drive right to your work but not sure you

Notes -
I was in the habit of trying to guess what would happen in situations and movies. The experiences I was having were so profound and mysterious; I wanted to know everything about them. I wanted to understand what I was going through and what it all meant. It's not so important for me to know all that now. All I need to know is the next step. It's hard to stay in that state because of the mysteries unfolding, but staying in the present moment serves best. It is a peaceful place.

Pa and I enjoyed eating ribs at a place called KC's Rib Shack. They have paper on the table along with a box of crayons, and you can draw on the paper on the table. The last time we ate there, we drew deer. Again, I don't eat meat anymore. I feel like Mother Ayahuasca has guided me not to eat meat. I see that it helps the Earth if I don't, so it makes sense that she would guide me in such a way.

I wanted to go straight to Pa and throw myself at his feet. I wanted him to know that I loved him above all else and that he was my king. I wanted him to know that

I saw his pure form and that I am in awe of all that he is. I wanted him to know that I would dedicate my life to making our life together as happy and peaceful as possible. I realized that others had not gone through what I did, and perhaps it may make him uncomfortable and look odd to his workmates. I opted to meet him at home.

Page 62:

<u>Transcript</u> -
8/31/15
would appreciate that. It would disturb your peace, I am sure.

Pa, I think we will make such great team when we are together again. I think maybe it would be good would be good for us if you tapped into your spirituality a little more. I believe you feel selfish but if you did for you (took care), you would take care of many.

I have been in my room all day. I am tired. It is exhausting talking all the time. I like to have quiet time some times. Doris told me to work on my self-esteem so I am banging out this book + going to make an action plan for the exercises.

Pa, as much as I believe I have to take this second "flight" on my own and feel the washuma showed me that, I still feel your love

Notes -
We were always a great team, but I was looking to improve and knew this shamanic cleanse would help me do that, on a whole other level.

It's hard to have all that clarity and feel like you are on top of the world and not want others to join you. Essentially, that is what this book is offering. It's not a guarantee, but most likely the experiences associated with meeting Mother Ayahuasca and being led to your higher self will lead to what feels like the top of the world. I want that for you. I know what suffering feels like, and needless suffering is the worst of it all. One may ask, you mean I don't have to feel like shit a good percentage of time? Absolutely not.

8/31/15
and support. I don't know why I feel nervous about doing it but I do. Thank you for being here for me. My new friend Heidi and I talked and we said who knows what the men in our lives are doing - they could be making plans with other women. I realize it would be best for me to be attached to neither. I do hope you miss me, love me, and are looking forward to reuniting with me. Papa, we are getting ready to take flight again. [I didn't get to this time] I am nervous, but ready. I have love in my heart. I hope I get to feel your presence (sp?) again. I love you, pa.

Second Aya Trip
9.1.15
Dear Husband (King), "They" told me you are.

I am here. I was correct about the 1st Aya being orientation. The "Bad" (great) Washuma trip was in preparation for last night's trip

Notes -
I felt like Pa with me, supporting and loving me. His words floated through my head and rested on my heart.

"They" could have been my guides or Mother Ayahuasca. I was just getting used to the idea of a plant communicating with me, at the time. The more fascinating thing is that she keeps communicating with me. I am not always clear about it when she does, but over time, I am able to determine that it is her, after the fact.

9/1/15
home. The ceremony was pretty much the same but the trip was completely different. Just as I could feel all the love in 1st trip, I felt all the pain, agony, and suffering in the second. I found out that I came to earth to learn + to help people. In my Earth life, I felt all the pain, agony, [it was scary as fuck] and suffering of Earth people. I chose to go to Earth with that as my mission. I did a great job, pa. You chose me. You

chose me because you can see me. Apparently, I am a pure heart? I am not entirely sure what that means. I am told my true name is Gloria. I wish I could Google it to see the meaning. Your name is Shem, I am told. Your name was purposely put in the Bible so your Earth parents would name you that. I made more connections of helpers, like the nun who gave me the book she "prayed"

I had a hard time believing that I am a PH. I had to settle into it. The process was interesting and I felt accepting of reality. It was weird.

I felt all the pain of those who were suffering in that room. I was told to help them, be a good example, and support them. It was scary but I did it.

Notes -

I am still unsure about what all this means, but I don't need to know. This is what I learned, and my life has been driven in the direction of helping more people. I was on the right path, and now I am helping even more people, on a deeper level. I have found that many people want to help others. Why? It seems that they too have gone through a hard time of their own.

I did feel all the pain and suffering, and I lay there and held space for my brothers and sisters. I sent energy out to them and called them brothers and sisters, in my mind. I said things like, "Let it out, sister, you can do it. I am here for you." That is what they told me to do: support and cheer others on. I think that is what I am to do in real time, on Earth, and I intend to do it. You can do it, brothers and sisters. You bought this book for a reason. Create your own hype, and see where it takes you. I had a hard time accepting that I am a good person and that I deserve to be happy. I learned to accept it during this experience, and for that and more, I am grateful. I felt "less than," before this trip. I didn't feel I was good enough for Pa, but then, why else would he choose me?

I was convinced that my name is Gloria, but I have a bit of doubt because of the number of times I use the word "glorious" to describe certain things in this journal. Was that in my mind or is it truth? I will tell you that I feel all "they" told me and all I learned is absolutely true. It is my truth. I am not sure how it all works and have many questions, but I believe.

9.1.15
on and put a place mark for a few pages that would help me along the way. They did. I felt so alone, for so long, and now, **I am free.**

This is all so fascinating. I am told to quit my job, totally. I must seek the owner of the ME Alpaca store. I think her name is Magda or something like Maria. She will help us, or me figure out how to open the store. If there is already a store, I am told to work there. "They" will see to our or my success. I am to help people out of the store. I will host "parlors" out of the store.

At some level, I knew some of this. I think you do too. You did so much to help me get to this place. I love you and honor you. I was told to tell the teachers (the shaman) I love and honor them as well as others. I was told to say "thank you, pure heart" to Coby + Ananda (the hosts) and kiss their forehead and said "I received this in love, and I return with love".

Notes -
I did feel like I was taken out of *The Matrix* when I came back from my second meeting with Mother Ayahuasca. It was incredible! The shaman and facilitators talked about "coming home." I felt like I had been home, a place of origin, and that this space on Earth was fabricated. And it seemed to be dual. I also felt like home was home in my real and true self.

I was skeptical of this because I wasn't finding a Maria. I followed the leads and clues, though, and one day, a woman named Marie, who was not the owner of a store but a sales manager, called me. She said she would help me because she used to own a store in Canada. We scheduled a call, and she answered all of my questions and said she was available for me whenever I needed guidance.

There is a feeling of my life being designed in a certain way. I feel like I saw this future or planned it.

9/1/15

Papa, Music was a big part of the healing. Jaya is the 600 year old guy. He is so "the light".

The woman in the photo is Marie, the owner of the retreat center. She is selling it and this guy, Luke (a master in training) is going to buy it. He came to the Shamanic Cleanse because he saw his friend Bonita post it on Facebook. When Marie saw Luke, she said he will be the one to buy it. She knew. He said he knew too. We drank Mama Aya at night this time. We were all laid out in the living room, COZY! It was totally dark after the last person drank. They waited 1/2 hour and then the music started.

Notes -

The coming back to the space, which I like to view as the "landing" back on Earth, was heavenly. There were so many components to it. Some people were singing, and others told stories. The shaman and musicians seem to be a part of the vessel. They carry you to the other side. It's so gentle and loving. There is a feeling of protection, the way a fuselage is safety for one carried in a plane. I am grateful.

Luke never bought the place. He was told it was not the right space for him.

Page 67:

9/1/15

This other musician, Nacho played many instruments for us. They played the whole night, through. Here, he is playing the next day. They are gifted and giving. The music helps with the travel, big time!

Speaking of, we have the runner up for Peru has got talent playing at our party tonight. This will be a hell of a closing ceremony. I could listen to Jaya play all day long. These folks are so giving with music.

The day was so chill, papa. I took a much needed nap. The artist, Chaquira came with his band and gave us a concert. It was insane. We danced and laughed. It was powerful.

Notes –
Nacho's proper name is Ignacio Rodriguez.

When I think about passion, there is no better display than those who played and sang for us while we journeyed with plant medicine. I am grateful for their gifts and giving.

Things wound down with the ceremony, and we cleaned up. I was walking on clouds all day. They held a space of a paradise. I was astounded about what I experienced and what I learned of myself. I was the happiest I had ever been in my life. I was of the belief that I could be this happy forever, if I remembered and chose it. That was great news.

Page 68:

Transcript -
9/1/15
They won 2nd in "Peru's Got Talent"
The concert
Amaru, Pumac, Kuntur
Serpent, Puma, Condor
The Inca trilogy represents balance + harmony of life

Page 69:

Transcript -
The shaman, Selva (Debora) After the 1st Aya trip I thanked her for the tools + that I am here to learn. She said "Welcome to the family" + gave me a big hug. Her mom is Doris (Dorice) who reads the coca leaves.

(Aussie dude) Jaya aka Jesus to some. He never did play the song for me but he did pay me a song he wrote the morning after Aya 2nd trip. It was beautiful. + thanked me for listening. lol

Jaya writes poetry and has produced an album with his beloved, under the name Jaya Saraswati, named *Wave of the Heart*. Their words and music may move you, since they moved me.

Page 70:

Transcript -
9/1/15
These are the plants used to make plant bath.

I am exhausted, pa. We really celebrated today. We had a feast! We had out concert. We had some chocolate. It was a hell of a party. I am chilling in my room with a cup of incredible chai tea. I get to start coming home tomorrow.

I will not be going to work. I want to come home and make bacon chili. I am going to unwind in my room and pack my stuff. It's 6:11 pm and I am ready for bed.

Pa, it's been a hell of a trip. I am so grateful. I am

[pull off leaves and boil in a big pot, outside.]

[In the evening we gathered to say final shares. I said I love and honor all. I thanked the teachers for all the tools. I said my mind was blown many times and how grateful I am to be a part of this all. I said I could see how my whole life had led me to this. I said a few other things. They gave us each one a bracelet and sang each one of our names + that they love us. (in a song) Te amo, Carla.]

[The mountain in the back of the house we stayed. Mt. Patchu Tuson.]

Notes -
The party we were thrown was fantastic. Laura, who was an incredible chef, among other things, was in the kitchen for most of the morning, preparing a feast. She was playing her tunes and whipping up a buffet fit for kings and queens, and that is how most were walking around. It seemed like we felt and looked regal. There was music, laughter, sharing of stories, wonderful things to eat, happiness, and peace. I got all that and then a cup of wonderful chai tea. The gifts kept on coming. I was in disbelief.

How does one express gratitude for all the gifts given? I think the best way is to share and to help others along their journey. That is another reason for this book. I had no idea I would publish this. Although I have quite a way to go on my journey, I believe this can help others on theirs. I don't need to know my end to know that meeting Mama Aya was a catalyst to getting me where I am meant to be.

Page 71

Transcript -
9/1/15
still learning but this is plenty of information, for now.

Pa, this dude Darren packed his backpack + we didn't hear from him all day. In the night, he emailed the facilitators back to tell them he was in the U.S. Homeboy hit the road, Jack. It was just before the 2nd Aya trip.

This is my last night here, pa, we do a cacao ceremony in the morning. I love you! Good night, husband. (king)

9.2.15
This morning we did the cacao ceremony. It was essentially a strong ass hot cocoa. I was told it was harsh on the liver and so just had a little and let the rest go. Doris

[It woke me up!]

Notes -
It was odd that someone else wanted to leave, which I strongly wanted to do. My thoughts and love were with him as well as others on the trip. We connected when I came home, and I am happy to know him.

Page 72:

Transcript -
9/2/15
said my knees are bad + my liver is a concern, so I have to watch it. We had a great yoga class and then breakfast to wrap up the whole experience. Pa, this woman (the mother of the trip) said I get the award for biggest transformation. That was this

morning while she and I were saying goodbye. People were saying I was beaming and my eyes look so much brighter. I wonder how you will see me.

Jaya sang a song called the hummingbird song. It was my favorite and many other's as well.

My new friend Rose wrote the lessons for me.

The hummingbird brings these 8 eight lessons <u>for us to arrive</u>
1) To have fun
2) To be free
3) is eternal happiness
4) Just be
5) stay strong
6) carry on
7) create heaven
8) don't wait!

<u>Notes</u> -
This song is off the hook and so simple. If I follow these simple rules, I am in heaven. Don't wait.

Page 73:

<u>Transcript</u>-
9/2/15
I saw a hummingbird when I was tripping balls on Washuma in the magical place near the hot springs. I realize now that each Washuma trip prepared me for each Aya trip. It's pretty fascinating and I am grateful. The first had me let go and know all is perfect and the second showed me darkness and that I would have to get through some things alone and it would be scary. The first also showed me the grid on my hand that looked like tattoo.

Pa, not everyone came through to the other side and was shown the way "home". I wonder why? Maybe they are not ready. I get the feeling/have intuition that women are more powerful "there".

Pa, after we came in for a landing, people were sharing wise tales/sayings. It was completely in the dark and there were about 4 people who kept shooting out these sayings + stories. It was cool as

Notes -
Looking back, it seems that this was the way it happened. I am grateful for the ease and power in which each teaching plant guided me. It was just what I needed.

I am not sure what that even means. Some people said they fell asleep and had a good rest or they had this vision or that. I talked to one person I was told about in my experience. After she told me some things, I told her I already knew it and added some details to corroborate the story. We were both in a bit of shock. I knew some of the things she went through because they told me. She was one of the ones I knew I was cheering on and why. It was incredible.

Page 74:

Transcript -
9/2/15
Shit! The musician, Nacho's wife said she had been to 100s of these Aya ceremonies and this was the best one she ever witnessed. We were all in the one space - living room + dinning room on mats on the floor with blankets all around. They gave us Rapey, eye drops, puke buckets, and toilet paper to get ready. Each is called up, one by one to receive mama Aya and then sent back to our spots. People take different doses. If they throw it up too fast, they take another dose.

I am tired as all hell. I am at the airport with only about six more hours to go until my flight to Atlanta. I am going to eat meat! I think I left my crystal at the center. Maybe it's in my back pack.

I was part of something very special, pa. I can't be more grateful!

Notes -
I *was* part of something very special. I *am* grateful beyond words. I honestly got through my king's cancer journey and was a source of strength and peace during my king's cancer journey it, mostly due to this experience. Where do I even begin to be grateful? How do I repay that? I can help other people as best I can, that's how.

<u>Transcript</u> -
9/2/15
lol, you should see me. I look like a god damn hippy Peruvian chick. I feel great though. I have something called "Aqua Florida". It is used to protect against bad energy. (I think) I see some in the airport where luggage is checked. I hope they don't take mine. I also have washuma infused chocolates - got two out of this plane ride. lol. I hope I don't fly too high. I simply want to relax.

Pa, there are all kinds of plant medicine. Mama (pacha) means earth mother. Mother Earth to be specific. Pacha mama. The symbol for her is something like.

She is honored and loved in Peru. + by me

I have never felt more real or existing in my life. I feel alive + free.

There were 14 of us "travelers" in total. One couple man + woman plus

<u>*Notes*</u> -
I look back and see wanting to sit with Huachuma this way as irresponsible and disrespectful.

This magical experience helped me connect with Mother Earth, find respect and honor for her, and view her as more than a place under my feet.

<u>Transcript</u> -
9/2/15
2 single men and the rest were women. Only the one dude bolted before the 2nd Aya trip. There were 2 powerful people - a woman + a man. "They" told me the woman is part of mama pacha and takes on people "shit". - their darkness. The man, "they" told mens powerful and is able to make time stand still. When I told them what "they" told me, it resonated with them. The woman "got" most of what i said and said "they" told her, her man was her king and she was to help him too. (like you are mine and I am to help you) WILD!!!

Pa, I can't just talk about this with anyone + I hope you won't talk about it openly either.

I think my favorite non-shaman bits were how they served mashed avocado with most meals and the private concert by Chaquira + his band.

I am still in shock!

Notes -
I guess that didn't stand. I had a feeling that it would be best to keep things quiet to maintain respect for Mama Ayahuasca. When I got home to the United States, I learned that many people who sat with her did not understand the shaman ways or respect or honor the plant medicine. It was much like people treat cannabis. I didn't like it. I mentioned that Mama Aya speaks long after you meet her. It's true, and she let me know that she didn't mind getting used, so that she could help the people of the Earth. That is another reason for this book. I have received guidance from my spirits, and they let me know that Peru wasn't for me and that I should "keep writing." I was focused on Pa's cancer journey at the time I was told, so I couldn't focus on much other than that. After he transitioned, a couple of friends who I was in ceremony with encouraged me to publish this journal. I also got word that more shaman are being trained and that Mama Aya doesn't want to keep it quiet anymore. I told this all to a friend, and she said Mama Aya let her know something similar. My objective was clear. That is how this offering came to be.

Page 77:

Transcript -
9/2/15
I was essentially taken out of the matrix. It felt like that - like I left my body. We are light. I am not afraid of anything anymore. AND, a lot of this earth stuff doesn't matter so much anymore. I hope you don't think I am crazy. LOL Salva was saying how these commercialized practices don't prepare people and that their minds explode. I can see how that can happen. Jaya said during yoga that one should surrender. I totally did! That makes things much easier. This is all so hard to believe. There seems to be truth in the movies - The Matrix and Avatar.

Chaquira brought his own crystals + stones to sell. He spotted my neck piece and said "The Shaman Stone ... Laboradorita." A couple of people noticed it. How weird is it that I have had this thing for over

Notes -

It made me happy to read this bit. It's how I felt, and I think I stated much of this in side notes, not realizing this was here. It's worth repeating. I was nervous to share this all with Pa. He was a bit insulted because he said he knew all about this stuff. He knew this is what some experience from what he had read, since he'd been studying this for over ten years. I was surprised, again. I asked him why he didn't tell me. He said that he didn't want to scare me. He was very proud of me for taking this journey, and at times he couldn't believe that I did it. His view was that not only did I do it, but I did it somewhat blindly, on a whim. He saw that I was drawn to it.

Page 78:

Transcript -
9/2/15
14 years + a couple of weeks before my trip, a random woman points out that it is Labradorite? There are so many things in my life that make sense now. I didn't wear anything during Aya ceremonies. Metal is supposed to interfere with energy.

Medicine song - The first I heard sung. It made me so happy because it reminds me of a Thich Nhat Han song.

Pacha Mama

Pacha Mama, I am coming home
to the place where I belong
(deleted because of IP laws)
(deleted because of IP laws)

I want to be free, so free
like the flowers and the bees
(deleted because of IP laws)
(deleted because of IP laws)

They played this song for us in the beginning of the trip. It was fast, a favorite. It wasn't until the end that I really understood that it has meaning for me. I am grateful.

Page 79:

Transcript -
9/2/15
I want to fly high, so high
Like the eagle in the sky
(deleted because of IP laws)
(deleted because of IP laws)

And when my time has come
(deleted because of IP laws)

There were so many great medicine songs. I liked the ones that sounded like Indian type songs. I am going to have to look them up. It was so cool, when were were in flight (many reported) that when the music was playing, it sounded like it was right over our heads.

Pa, I am still processing all of this. It seems unbelievable! What if it is all bullshit? LOL, what if I just got high as a motherfucker and my mind did the rest? Salvia makes people have similar experiences. I got to figure

Notes -
What if? What, who, when, where ... I had and have so many questions and want to know everything. Meditation and Buddhist teachings came in very handy for this time in my life. All I have to do is breath and stay in the present moment, and the rest takes care of itself. There is still a lot of mystery, and things have happened to me since that are hard to believe, which makes all that happened on this journey more believable, but I don't have to have all the answers right away. "They" told me, "The journey is heaven," and I agree.

Transcript -

9/2/15

this shit out. It's the shift. It's the awakening. If it's true that we make our own story, I want this one. There is no pain "there", only love. It's quite beautiful! Pa, I felt home. I felt connected to all my "brothers and sisters". It's one connection and the love flows so powerfully.

9/3/15

I am watching a bad movie about a couple who are aging and meet a younger, hip couple. The younger couple invites them to an Aya ceremony. They make it seem like it is just to get high and hallucinate + puke + puke + puke. It's an awful portrayal.

I looked at the photos your sister sent to me. I started crying. The photos show exactly how the grid and all that seems to be. It's interesting and a bit funny that the shaman talk about taking a flight. They ask about (or screen)

Notes -

I love my story, for me. It's perfect for me. It has had its tough times and great times. I can see experiences as lessons and not get attached to them or take them personally. It's been great to take what I have learned into my everyday life.

Page 81:

Transcript -

9/3/15

folks taking prescription drugs. They say that is the TSA. LOL. They need to know so they can adjust the plant medicine dose or some can't take, depending.

I want to email the dude who jetted so he doesn't feel bad. He left around 4 in the morning and left a lot of his shit, including his suitcase. He put together a back pack and was out. He must have gotten SPOOKED!!!

Holy cow! At the airport out of Cusco to Lima, I was telling this lady that a highlight was seeing Chaquira play. She asked if he/they played any Beatles. What? No, but I wish I knew. How cool is that? I should have worn my shirt that day.

About to land in Boston. Let the beginning begin. I hope it begins with me getting home with no overheated car.

~Aho!~

Notes -
When I read the close of this page, I didn't know why I ended this way, but after some thought, I recalled it's because of this Beatles song. I will share a few of the last lines of the lyrics to "Tomorrow Never Knows," by the Beatles:

"Or play the game
'Existence' to the end
Of the beginning
Of the beginning."

I am grateful! I love you, Pa!

The beginning

About the Author

Carla Mora lives in Unity, NH. She spent most of her life living in Boston, MA where she had a challenging childhood. It led to her working on personal development with passion, for many years. When her love became ill, she left the business world behind after sixteen years and is currently pursuing a career as a health coach and reiki practitioner. Through her experiences with plant medicine, people, and reading, she has found that her passion is to help people.

Printed in the United States
By Bookmasters